JUVENILES IN TROUBLE

RICHARD WORMSER

JULIAN MESSNER

PUBLISHED BY SIMON & SCHUSTER

New York   London   Toronto   Sydney   Tokyo   Singapore

In memory of my Aunt Sophie

PHOTO ACKNOWLEDGMENTS:

Covenant House: page 18 (photo by Kenneth Siegel);
pages 32, 45, 147 (photos by George Wirt); pages 26, 42, 145.

Allain Jullien: page 40.

Stock • Boston: pages 67, 72 (photo by Steve Starr).

Richard Wormser: pages 10, 13, 16, 25, 29, 77, 78, 82, 87, 108, 110, 111, 113, 116 (top and bottom), 117, 121, 131, 133, 135, 140, 141.

JULIAN MESSNER
Published by Simon & Schuster
1230 Avenue of the Americas
New York, New York 10020
Copyright © 1994 by Richard Wormser
All rights reserved including the right of reproduction in whole or in part in any form.
JULIAN MESSNER and colophon are trademarks of Simon & Schuster.
Designed by Greg Wozney
Manufactured in the United States of America
10 9 8 7 6 5 4 3 2 1

Library of Congress Cataloging-in-Publication Data
Wormser, Richard.
  Juveniles in trouble / by Richard Wormser.
    p. cm.
  Includes bibliographical references and index.
  1. Juvenile delinquency—Juvenile literature. [1. Juvenile
delinquency.] I. Title.
HV9069.W67 1994 364.3′6—dc20 93-35899 CIP AC
ISBN: 0-671-86775-X

CONTENTS

JUVENILES IN TROUBLE

Introduction

In an average day in the lives of America's troubled youth, nine will die by guns; six will commit suicide; twenty-seven will die from causes related to poverty; almost three thousand unmarried girls will become pregnant; 623 teens will become infected with venereal disease or AIDS; almost 1500 will drop out of school; close to two thousand will be sexually abused; more than three thousand will run away from home; and nearly 1700 will end up in jail.

Juveniles in Trouble presents a dramatic portrait of America's most troubled and troublesome teenagers. In this book, you will meet runaway and throwaway kids, single mothers, drug dealers and users, prostitutes, car thieves, robbers, and killers. You will meet teenagers who hit bottom and stay there, and others who slowly and painfully pull themselves up by their bootstraps, with the help of a variety of people and programs.

Juveniles in Trouble reveals what happens to young people who try to survive on the streets and become caught up in a life of crime. The book takes the reader on a tour of the underworld of teenage gangs and drug dealing. It enters the doors of the criminal justice system and follows, step by step, the legal process as it develops from arrest to detention, trial, sentencing, probation, and incarceration. *Juveniles in Trouble* shows how both the adult and juvenile court systems work, from the prosecutor's and judge's point of view as well as the defendant's. You will learn why some convicted youths are sent to jail and others are placed on probation. You will see programs that have been designed to turn kids around including both private residences and prison facilities such as boot camps.

Juveniles in Trouble also examines juveniles who kill and what happens to them when they get caught. Every year, approximately 1200 murders are committed by teenagers. The penalties can be harsh: life imprisonment for some; death for others. The book also visits death row to present a gripping portrait of men sentenced to death for crimes committed when they were juveniles. Disturbing questions are raised about what should be done with those who commit both violent and nonviolent crimes. Is rehabilitation possible? Is it preferable? Or is it more important to punish?

Juveniles in Trouble also examines several programs that help teenagers get their lives on track. It shows what it is like to be in a Covenant House Crisis center, a group home, a drug program and on probation. It also describes the therapeutic process and shows how it works.

Juveniles in Trouble examines the relationship between family breakdown and juvenile crimes. It offers a description of places where young people can turn for help before it is too late, places where their confidences will be kept. But this book does not offer any easy solutions to the complex problems of so many of America's young people. Nor can it safely predict whether or not America will solve the problems that lead to juveniles in trouble.

A street kid. Approximately one million young people leave or are thrown out of their homes every year.

1

RUNAWAY AND THROWAWAY KIDS

The Outreach van eased out of the Covenant House garage and onto the streets of the city. It was ten P.M., the hour when tens of thousands of runaway and throwaway kids begin to appear on the streets of New York. It is a world seldom seen by most people. "It is a whole subculture created by street kids," says Teri Thorpe, driver of the van. "When the sun comes up, it dissipates. You don't see it anymore."

Teri Thorpe is an Outreach worker for Covenant House, the largest private organization in the United States designed to help young people in trouble. Covenant House provides a variety of services for youths, ranging from offering a sandwich and a soft drink to a hungry street kid to an intensive drug therapy program for young addicts. Covenant House also offers short-term residence to juveniles in trouble and long-term programs where young people learn trades, find jobs, and finish their education.

Most of the young people Teri Thorpe meets are lost to the streets. Many are sad, hopeless, and often helpless. They include young boys and girls hustling change for a meal, selling their bodies, shoplifting, and mugging. They are teenagers like Ralph, a high school sophomore who was abused by his adoptive father from the age of three. He left home at fourteen. He says, "Family life hurts so much. I just put myself to where I couldn't feel anymore: so I don't

In New York City and other urban centers, Covenant House Outreach workers offer food and help to young people living on the streets.

feel." Or Kate, the fifteen-year-old girl who attempted suicide and who likes to show her scars: "This is where I tried to kill myself, the night before last. I was sticking myself with a safety pin. I told my friend and she thought it was gross. But it didn't even hurt. A razor blade hurts for a long time." Then there is Ben, orphaned at fourteen, who, in order to survive, made a decision: "I could sell my body or rob old ladies. I didn't want to sell my body."

These kids live from door to door, trick to trick, friend to friend," Teri Thorpe says. Many turn to drugs in an attempt to escape the misery, discomfort, and absence of love in their lives. Some form "family" groups and live together in abandoned buildings or other sites.

Mark, fifteen, who lives in an underground cave with other street kids says, "We've all adopted each other. I've got more of a family orientation than I have with my real family." If they are in their early teens or younger, and reasonably attractive, the youngsters will often "work" for adults who viciously exploit them sexually.

Every year, an estimated 1 million children under the age of eighteen either run away or are thrown out of their homes. The average age of a street kid is fifteen years old. About half are girls. Eighty percent are white. More than half have been physically and sexually abused. They are also victims of neglect, abandonment, emotional mistreatment, and inadequate or malicious parents. Some feel they have no choice other than to run away. Some are too ashamed to tell how they were abused. Others fear what will happen to them if they tell.

Not every runaway is physically abused at home. Some teenagers are well treated by their parents but still have difficulty adjusting to the rules at home. Deeply alienated from the world, restless and bored by everything around them, they gravitate to the street and toward others who are as alienated as they. One girl found herself gradually dropping out of everything, including her family:

The friends I got didn't belong to anything. I was accepted with the burnout kids because I was a burnout, pure and simple. I was punk and I used to dress wicked wild. A lot of things I did weren't accepted by a lot of people, but in the burnout crowd, you could kill your mother and father and they wouldn't care. If you didn't do drugs, you weren't in the burnout crowd, if you didn't do a lot of stuff, you weren't in it, and you were a nerd. I'd rather be a burnout than a nerd.

At one time runaways were hunted by the police and were harshly treated by the law. They were considered "incorrigible" by the courts and were often sent to jail, where they were brutalized, learned to become career criminals, or sometimes were murdered. Many were returned to their parents. Today, the police tend to ignore street kids if they are not breaking the law or, if they need help, will try to put them in touch with places that can assist them. While most street kids are suspicious of government agencies, they tend to trust private organizations such as Covenant House. Workers like Teri Thorpe neither judge street kids nor try to convince them to change their lives. Teri's first task is to let street kids know that Covenant House is there for them: "Many kids are suspicious and it takes a while to build up their trust. We want to get them off the streets if we can, but we also want to make sure that they're all right, that they don't need anything at the moment, that they have some food in them. Just keeping them alive is often a major victory."

The Outreach van cruises through areas where young people congregate at night. Some areas are highly dangerous, such as Hunts Point in the Bronx, the grocery wholesale market where much of the city's groceries are distributed and where teenagers sell drugs and sex openly. Once, a fourteen-year-old boy, concerned about the safety of the Covenant House workers, offered Teri a chance to protect herself and her colleagues. "You guys want some guns?" he asked. "I can get 'em for you real cheap. You should have something out here." The workers thanked him for his concern but, declining, offered him some food instead.

The van cruises the meat district in lower Manhattan where transvestites, some as young as fourteen, dress in women's clothes and work as "female" prostitutes. Kim, a young Vietnamese transvestite, stops to chat with Teri while keeping one eye out on the street for the police and the other for customers. Kim regards himself as a woman and is dressed in a tight, black miniskirt, a halter top, and high heels. Teri asks Kim if he is practicing safe sex. Kim shrugs at the question and says that customers pay more for unprotected sex. The money Kim earns is used to support a two hundred–dollar a day drug habit. Safe sex is virtually unknown on these streets. And as these teenagers grow into young adults, one can see in their gaunt faces, feverish eyes, and thin bodies the outward manifestations of AIDS.

Many street kids regard Teri as a counselor-parent. They tell her news about what's happening on the streets, their troubles with boyfriends and girlfriends, their medical problems. Teri listens, but does not support their illusions. "We send the message, 'We're not judgmental; we're here to help you. But we can't applaud your fantasies.' If a kid is acting high and says he's drunk on champagne, we tell him, 'Listen, alcohol is a depressant. But you seem wired. Like

Covenant House Outreach Worker Teri Thorpe tries to persuade a young woman with medical problems to see a doctor.

you're high." Teri admits it is hard to get street kids to give up their life-style. "The younger you get the kid, the better chance you have of saving them." As Jim Harness, chief operating officer of Covenant House, pointed out:

> **The street becomes an addiction in itself, the excitement or whatever it is. All the money in the world would not get all these kids off the street.**

Teri adds that even violence is not enough to convince young people to leave the streets:

> **Sometimes you think if a kid has a bad experience, he'll give it up. But they've been shot, they've been mugged, and they're right back there in the same location doing the same thing. Their level of tolerance rises until they are faced with actually losing their life. After that, there are no more levels.**

The most difficult youths to help on the street are teenage female prostitutes. Many are runaways who became involved with men who promised them love and friendship, but turned out to be pimps. Pimps have warned Covenant House workers to stay away from "their" girls and at times have punctuated their warnings by shooting a window out in the van. Teri says:

> **You never see the adults behind the kids who are doing it. You never see the pedophile, the pimp. So you go to talk to a kid and suddenly you have a number of adults who are looking at you affecting their livelihood. So there's a danger in that.**

Many of these teenage girls live in a state of constant terror of their pimps and can only work when numbed by drugs. It is too painful for many of them to think of their former lives. One girl, forced to work the streets on Christmas Eve, said she began to think of her life at home as a child and, remembering the good times she once had, began to cry and couldn't stop. "I've got to stop crying," she told herself. "Nobody is going to buy me if I'm crying. It wrecks a john's fantasy when a kid he wants to buy has tears in her eyes."

Another group of street kids difficult to help are drug addicts. All too often they love their drugs too much to be helped. Many, like Douglas, have been on the streets from a very young age. Both of Douglas's parents were drug addicts. His father served time in jail. Before his father was incarcerated, Douglas lived in a number of hip-

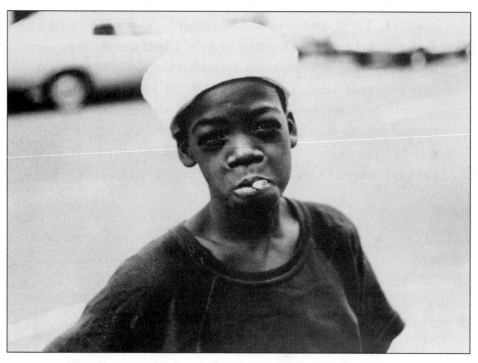

Most of today's "street kids" are homeless children abandoned by their families rather than runaways.

pielike communes throughout the country as his parents fled from the police. At the age of thirteen, Douglas left home. For the next two years, he lived on the streets, hitchhiking from place to place, and stealing to live. His ultimate destination was the Strip in Los Angeles, a section of the city marked by bars and restaurants, neon lights, and coffee shops. Here thousands of young people hang out, attracted by the warm climate, the glamour of Hollywood, drugs and sex.

The first few months on the Strip for Douglas were almost fatal. Street workers found him huddled on a stoop, half dead from drugs and malnutrition. They placed Douglas in a homeless shelter where he met other homeless kids who taught him how to survive on the streets:

> **The runaways took a liking to me. They were cool. They were fifteen to sixteen years old. They had respect. They were rock and rollers. And I loved it. I met a girl. I learned how to hustle. I learned how to go in the back of restaurants, run in, take something and run out real fast. I learned how to steal from soda machines. We lived in an empty warehouse. They taught me so much about drugs. Weed, uppers, acid. I was selling acid. I looked twelve. When I got busted, I said my parents were dead. So they wouldn't lock me up.**

At the age of fifteen, Douglas fell in with a poetry/drug counter-culture that resembled the beat generation of the 1950s. He discovered his love and talent for poetry and became "hooked into the poetry scene." He also began to shoot heroin and take pills to "get down with these people." His life began to deteriorate:

> **I was selling myself to get drugs. I was getting high, getting arrested and getting diseased. Hepatitis B.**

Mental institutions. I knew two ways of life: junky life on the street, and institution life, locked away. I didn't know community life.

Douglas finally took steps to turn his life around. He was one of the few street kids who had the courage to admit that his way of life led to either a mental institution, prison, or death. Another was Kelly, now nineteen, once a throwaway kid.

Until she was nine, Kelly lived with her parents. Her life was extremely regimented. "When I was nine my room wasn't like a kid's room. It was like a guest room." One day, she went to school after her mother beat her. "I once went to school with a handprint on my face and they found out how I was being treated. Mother always said it was my fault. She agreed to give me up to foster care."

For the next nine years, Kelly shuttled among fifty foster homes. Foster care, she admits, did not work out for her. Much of the time, the fault was hers:

I knew who my parents were. All I wanted was to be where they were, even though I wasn't too happy with my mother and she wasn't too happy with me. What I wanted was a home—something of my own, something that was mine. That was the part that rebelled against my being in foster homes.

When Kelly was eighteen, she lived with friends for awhile. But she knew her welcome was limited: "Who wants to bother with you when you have problems? When you have problems, nobody wants to know you." Eventually she turned to the streets:

I used to sleep in the park at night. Nighttime wasn't bad. I always slept with one eye open. People would ask me, "Ain't you afraid to sleep in the park at

**night?" I tell them, Ain't you afraid to take the sub-
way during the day?" More stuff happens during the
day than at night. Even the crazy people go to sleep.**

Kelly tried to renew contact with her mother, thinking that now
that she was older, her mother might welcome her back. "Once when
I was down and out I called her and she said, 'well, there's always
public assistance.'" The experience depressed Kelly so much she
thought of suicide. But drawing upon her own inner resources, she
sought help and began to change her life:

**A couple of years ago, I wanted to end it all. You got
to look at the good things, though. Okay, I'm homeless, but I'm now getting the opportunity to go to college. If I had done myself in a couple years ago, I
wouldn't have had this opportunity. Maybe my life was
hard, but there are always people less fortunate than
me. You got to look at it that way. Or you'll never get
ahead. It gave me a chance to make something of
myself. If I had really gone ahead and killed myself,
I'd've never gotten opportunities.**

Kelly found help at Covenant House, one of the many shelters
that exist in the United States for street kids. Some go there to seek
temporary refuge from the storms of life and then return to the night-
mare existence from which they have not had the strength to escape.
But others, like Kelly and Douglas, seek to abandon their life on the
streets and anchor themselves securely in the world.

2

SHELTER FROM THE STORM

Two A.M. Janice is standing on the curb looking scared and lonely. She is dressed in a skimpy dress and wearing bright red lipstick and high heels. Cars pass by, slow down, stop. Prices are discussed, the cars move on.

Nearby, a Covenant House Outreach van is parked with two counselors inside. From time to time, Janice glances at the van. She wants to walk over, yet she's terrified that if she does, somebody might see her. Finally, during a moment when the street is empty, she summons up her courage and approaches.

The driver of the van offers her a sandwich and some lemonade. Janice eagerly accepts. The driver asks Janice if she would like to sit in the van a few minutes and rest. A look of terror crosses her face. "Maybe in a couple of hours," she says. "Will you be around in a couple of hours?" Her voice is pleading. As she speaks, she keeps glancing up and down the street. If she is seen talking to the Covenant House workers her life will be in danger. Her pimp guards his prostitutes closely. Young girls like Janice earn thousands of dollars a week for him.

The driver of the van gently urges Janice to enter. She finally yields.

"Only for a minute or two," she says, "then I got to go. My boyfriend will be really mad if he finds out I'm doing this."

"Your 'boyfriend'?" the driver asks.

"Yeah, he told me he doesn't want me talking to you guys. So I can't stay long. Can I have another sandwich? I'm really hungry."

"Sure. But why do you call him your boyfriend if he lets you walk the streets at night? Do you mean your pimp?"

Janice protests that her "boyfriend" truly loves her. She shows off the cheap jewelry he bought her to prove his love. But her defenses are beginning to crumble. Soon she is in tears: "I'm scared. I'm really scared. Do you think you can help me? My boyfriend beats me up if I don't do what he tells me. I think I'm pregnant. What am I going to do?"

For the next twenty minutes, Janice tells her story. It is a familiar one to the workers. Born and raised in a small town in the Midwest, she has run away from home after a bitter argument with her parents. Arriving in New York and not knowing anyone, she met a man at a bus station. He promised to take care of her, which he does for a few weeks. Then he demands that she pay him back for his favors. She has no choice. The only fortunate thing that has happened is that her "boyfriend" has not yet forced her to take drugs. This is a way many pimps keep their "girls" under control.

The workers ask Janice how old she is. She looks at least seventeen. Janice hesitates. "Fourteen."

She then asks the Covenant House workers to help her escape. Despite the risks, the workers do not hesitate. The driver of the van pulls away and heads toward the Covenant House Crisis Center, where Janice will be safe and helped to start a new life.

Originally, Covenant House was the only place where runaway teenagers in trouble like Janice could find immediate refuge and help. It was founded by Father Bruce Ritter, a Franciscan priest who, until 1964, was a professor of medieval theology at Manhattan College in New York. Driven by a deep need to "live and work among the poor," Father Ritter moved from a comfortable university environment into a roach-infested tenement house in the East Village of New York, an area infamous for its drug addicts and petty criminals. Father Ritter, who preferred to be called Bruce, supported himself by teaching, driving a cab, and working as a part-time minister. He recruited several other priests to help him with his mission.

According to Father Ritter, in the early morning hours of a bitter cold winter's night in February of 1970, four boys and two girls, all under sixteen years of age, appeared at his door and asked if they could stay there. Father Ritter agreed to let them sleep on the floor for the night.

Soon, the number of runaways began to grow and Father Ritter had no space for them in his overcrowded apartment. He began to take over other apartments in his building that had been vacated by junkies who had either died, got arrested, or just disappeared. By 1972, Father Ritter had managed to receive enough donations to set up Covenant House as an ongoing organization with its own buildings. Father Ritter explained Covenant House's mission in his book, *Covenant House: Lifeline to the Streets:*

Kids come to Covenant House because they have no place to go. Most are in flight from deplorable living conditions, hungry and scared. Some are in flight from themselves. The problem for all of them is very simple. Where am I going to sleep tonight? Or eat tonight? Who will take care of me tonight?

Today, Covenant House has established itself in eleven major cities in the United States, and has facilities in Canada, Mexico, and Central America. Every year, 25,000 young people enter Covenant House facilities seeking food, shelter, and a safe place to stay. Many of them will return to the life that brought them there. But a large number do use the resources that Covenant House provides as a means to reorganize their lives.

The largest crisis center is in New York City. It is an eight-story building located on 41st Street and 10th Avenue. Approximately 300 people can be sheltered there. Most residents are homeless young people from the city rather than runaways from out of town. Twenty-four hours a day, seven days a week, homeless and runaway young people enter asking for shelter, food, and help. For many the youth shelter is a beacon in a dark, violent world. And if they are between the ages of twelve and twenty-one, Covenant House will provide it without hesitation.

It is eleven-thirty in the morning. Ibrahim, an intake counselor, is on duty at the intake desk. It is his job to process the requests of young people applying for admission. He is a devout Muslim with a full beard, who has been working at Covenant House five years. Since he is the first worker young people meet when they enter Covenant House, he must reassure these often frightened and troubled youths that they are safe.

Day in and day out, an endless stream of young people ask to be admitted to the Covenant House Crisis Center: teen mothers with

New York City's Covenant House Crisis Center is located in the heart of Manhattan.

babies, drug addicts, sexually and physically abused boys and girls, children unable to get along with their parents, teens on the run from the law or from others seeking to harm them.

Chad is from Albany. Seventeen years old, small and blonde, he is without baggage. His back pocket has been ripped open with a knife. While asleep in a bus station, someone robbed him by cutting his pocket open and taking his money. His backpack was also stolen. A police officer directed him to Covenant House, where he sits in the office of Ibrahim, who will screen Chad and see what he can do to help him. Chad is scared of being here but even more scared of being out on the streets. Several times, he has been sexually approached by men while on the streets.

Chad explains to Ibrahim that his parents are separated. His mother disappeared several years ago and he was living in upstate New York with his father, an alcoholic who beat him. Last week, he

Covenant House is open 24 hours a day in eleven major cities in the United States.

threw Chad down a flight of stairs. Unwilling to accept the abuse, Chad left and came to New York.

Ibrahim tells Chad that he is welcome to stay at Covenant House. "Normally," Ibrahim explains, "we try to see if we can reconcile children with their families." A look of pain and fear crosses Chad's face. "However," Ibrahim reassures him, "when a parent has been as abusive as your father has, we don't do that. But we do have to let some member of your family know that you're safe. And if you're under eighteen, we have to report the abuse to the Children's Social Service Agency." Chad agrees to this condition.

As Ibrahim finishes with Chad, Michelle arrives, dragging two bags filled with all her possessions. She is eighteen, although her petite size and childish face make her look fourteen. This is her second visit to Covenant House.

Michelle explains her problems. They began when she and her mother began to have violent quarrels over whom she was dating, her staying out late and her grades in school. When she dropped out of school in the tenth grade, her mother was furious. "Me and my mom are like day and night," Michelle says. "I love her. I love her till it hurts me. I just don't like her."

When Michelle was eighteen, she started dating a man in his early twenties. She came home late at night, adding to the tension between her and her mother. "I was eighteen and I wanted to do what I wanted to do," Michelle says. Finally, Michelle stayed out all night with her boyfriend. When she returned home the next day, she found her bags packed and by the door. She was kicked out of the house with nowhere to go.

At first, Michelle started to stay with friends but the arrangement proved unsatisfactory in the long term. Michelle soon began to look elsewhere for a place to live.

You can only stay so long with friends and then they get tired of you. I began to live in and out of shelters.

**Slept in cars. I finally decided to come to Covenant
House and finish school and get a job. I had heard that
they do that for you.**

Michelle decided to change her life but while at Covenant House
she met a boy and they decided to live together. Michelle left to start
a new life with a man she believed loved her and would eventually
marry her. But her "boyfriend" had other ideas. He had no intentions
of finding a job. He pressured Michelle to make money fast. Without
skills, the only way open to a young, attractive girl to make "good
money" was in the sex industry. She began to work as a nude dancer,
and was soon making over a hundred dollars a night. "The money's
easy and quick but you lose your morals and your self-respect,"
Michelle says. Although she did not admit it, Covenant House workers believed she was on the verge of being pushed into prostitution
by her boyfriend.

Two things happened that made Michelle reconsider her life. Her
boyfriend began to beat her and she became pregnant:

**I always wanted to have a baby, but I didn't think I
was going to get pregnant. I wanted to believe he
wanted to be with me and we were going to get mar-
ried.**

Michelle soon realized that she was in a dead-end relationship
and things would only become worse. Because she feared her
boyfriend might kill her if he found out she was leaving him, Michelle
returned to Covenant House late one night without telling him.

For the next several days Michelle literally hid inside the Crisis
Center. She had decided to have her baby, but was unfocused about
her life and how she was going to support herself. She was also in
danger from her ex-boyfriend. The Covenant House staff decided to
move Michelle late at night to a "safe house," a place whose location

A Covenant House counselor helps a resident prepare her portfolio to apply to an art school. Residents of Covenant House may stay for as long as three months provided they make an effort to put their lives together.

nobody but a few staff members would know of. She could stay there until she had her baby, and try to start her life over again.

As she looks back at the mistakes she made, Michelle reflects:

> **I should have stuck to my original plan. If I had to do it all over again, I wouldn't have left. I would have stayed at Covenant House the first time and finished my education and gotten a job and not have gotten involved with this man. Now, I'm looking for another chance to start over again.**

During one interview, Ibrahim was interrupted by a phone call from a man claiming to be the stepfather of a missing child who insisted on knowing whether or not he was there. Ibrahim refused to give him any information:

> **I'm sorry, we can't give out that information. . . . That's our policy. We have to protect the residents here. It doesn't matter if you're his stepfather. If you give me your name and your phone number, I'll tell him you called, *if* he is here. I want to make it clear. I don't know whether or not he is here. I'm only saying that I'll pass your message to him if he is.**

Sometimes young people who ask for refuge are wanted by the police. Generally Covenant House will not allow anyone to remain until their legal problems are resolved. However, they will provide legal counsel to help settle the problem. Once admitted to the Covenant House Crisis Center, a young person will be sent to the unit most appropriate for his or her age and sex. Boys and girls live separately and are subdivided by age, with those under eighteen and over eighteen living on separate floors. All residents at Covenant House are assigned a counselor to help and guide them. They can also receive medical and psychiatric treatment, which will remain available to them even after they leave. The Crisis Center is a temporary residence where young people are helped to plan for more stable living arrangements. Some residents remain only a few days, others, a few months. But sooner or later all will leave, most of them hopefully to start a better life.

Covenant House has its regulations. Father Ritter liked to call them "commitments." Pat White, a former counselor, notes, "A lot of them [teenagers] ran away because of the rules. But wherever they go, they have to have rules." The basic rules are no weapons, no drugs, no fighting, and no sexual activity. There is also a routine that must be followed. Every weekday, residents rise at six o'clock to shower, dress, and clean their rooms. Then the rooms are locked. Breakfast is at eight. The younger residents will go to school during the day. Older residents may also attend school or go on a job search. Most are expected to look for jobs with the goal of becoming independent and having their own apartments. Covenant House teaches its residents how to look for a job and provides them with carfare to do so.

Sometimes residents try to beat the system. Angela, who has fled a sexually abusive stepfather, has been called into the staff office. For the past week, she has been given train fare to Long Island, where she says she is looking for a job and eventually wants to live. The staff has discovered that she has been hanging out on the streets instead of looking for work. Angela is warned not to try this again and is given another chance. If she repeats, she will be asked to leave. Three days later, Covenant House discharges her, but first finds a shelter to take her in so she won't have to live on the streets. Angela is also told that if she decides to seriously look for work, she can return to Covenant House for another chance.

Many juveniles, like Crissie, are highly motivated. She arrived at Covenant House late one night from California completely broke. Eighteen years old, born in North Carolina, and white, Crissie claims she has been living in China for six years. Although she speaks broken English, the staff is skeptical, but has no way of confirming her story. Crissie makes it clear to them that she is going to get a job as soon as possible and get her own place. "I need work eight hours," she explains. "Money, food, apartment, you know. Pay for language school. Want to be interpreter. Life is hard. I like to be independent. This time, I stuck. Stuck. This place good. But people here are different from me. I need my own place." The day after she arrives, Crissie has a job. Three days later, she finds a room to rent and is gone. No one ever learns whether or not she truly was from China.

Counseling is a large part of the services offered to teenagers. Every floor is staffed with at least two counselors to whom the resi-

Students are encouraged to finish their high school training and go on to college.

dents can come for advice. One evening, Donna enters the counselor's office on the older girls' unit. She is depressed and wants to talk to Pat, one of the counselors.

"I want to have an abortion," Donna says. She is six months pregnant. Because Covenant House is a Catholic institution, counselors cannot discuss abortion with the residents and must send them elsewhere for advice. However, Pat, being an experienced counselor, senses that abortion is not the real issue.

"What's wrong?"

Donna is silent for a moment. "Tell me," she suddenly cries out, "why can a woman be faithful but a man can't?"

Pat laughs. "Honey, if I had the answer to that one, I would be a millionaire."

Donna smiles. "I haven't been with another man since I met him. Now I learn he's gotten another woman pregnant."

"Maybe it's better you find out now than later. You know what I mean?"

Donna nods. Two days later she leaves without telling anyone where she is going.

There is little that Covenant House can do for those who have little desire to do anything for themselves. But for those young people who want to change their lifestyles, they can offer the tools to make the change. Monifa, nineteen, came to Covenant House after having discipline problems with her parents:

I wanted to do what I wanted to do. I lived with my father. I was raised a Muslim. I had to go to school with my head covered. I wanted to show my hair. When I went to school, I took off the head piece. Before I went back home, I put it on. I wanted to wear stylish clothes. Calvin Klein sneakers. My father wanted me home at a certain time, so I said, fine, I can go live with my mother. She didn't have no

rules or no curfew. And I loved it. But me being so lazy, I dropped out of school. I dropped out because of boys. I was trying to get attention from everybody. I tried to hang out with guys. I never had the guts to sell drugs. I never had the guts to sell my body. I was too scared. Now I regret dropping out of high school. I'll never have a prom. My prom! My prom! Seeing the girls get dressed up all pretty. A limo. I've never been in a limousine.

Monifa eventually joined the Job Corps in Virginia and lived with her boyfriend. But her temper got her in trouble. She got into a fight and injured a girl who brought charges against her. Monifa foolishly told the judge that she felt like killing the girl. The judge sent her to jail:

I was in jail for three days. It felt like a year. It felt so long. I was fined forty-six dollars and given a year probation. I learnt my lesson. I don't like jail at all. When you get angry, you don't think about anything. I didn't think about education, about family.

After her experience with jail, Monifa eventually returned to New York and began to see her life for what it really was:

I saw homeless people living on the street and I said I'm not going to be like them. I've got to do something with my life because I'm not going to be wasted like that, wake up one day and I'm twenty-five or thirty and living in a shelter.

Monifa came to Covenant House highly motivated to change her life. The discipline was hard. Getting up at six and spending the day searching for work was difficult for her. Having to live in a structured environment with curfews was even harder. But eventually Monifa found a job and planned to move into another Covenant House residence, where she will live while she works and completes her education.

Sister Mary Rose McGeady, the president of Covenant House, believes the task of helping runaway children today is harder than when Covenant House was founded.

> **The six thousand children who come to Covenant House every year have no protective environment. For many of them, nobody cares if they live or die. They lack the shelter of the family, the church, or the school—institutions that protect children. And in many cases, the family becomes the child's worst enemy. I remember one young man who ran away who said, "I just quietly walked away from hell."**
>
> **We try to provide that protection as best we can. We know many of the kids who come here live in hopelessness. They have not had success in their life. In fact, they may have been trained to fail. They have given up. Our job is to give them hope, to show them that they can succeed—one small step at a time. We get them to go back to school or get their GED. We help them find a job. We get them psychiatric help if they need it. And some of them do make it.**

What often helps young people like Monifa is the relationships they build with the staff. For many young people who have been deprived of the warmth of human relations, staff members often become the parents they never had. This human contact, although often brief, can sometimes make the difference between life and death, as one former homeless teenager revealed in a letter to the staff of Covenant House after she left to start a new life:

Dear Staff,

I would like to thank you all for everything you have done for me. When I first came to Covenant House, I was lost and afraid. I was very confused and ready to give up on life. Now, thanks to you all, I am much better, especially mentally. I've learned the real meaning of life. If I would have ended my life, I would have never met you all. I love each and every one of you. You are beautiful people. God bless you all. I love you. And remember me always.

> **Love Always,**
> **Helen**

But for some who make their way to Covenant House, reclaiming their lives is hard, and many obstacles have to be overcome before they can achieve success.

3

OVERCOMING ADDICTION

The ambulance sped through the streets of New York, its lights flashing, its sirens wailing. Cars in its path quickly pulled over to the side as the ambulance rushed past. Inside, Bernie was convinced he was dying. He thought that he had taken his last cocaine trip:

> I had been getting high when I felt my hand start getting numb. My arm started buggin' out. My chest felt like a football. I passed out. I woke up and saw gray, then things got darker and darker. My heart was going real fast—then real slow—then real fast. I said, "Bernie, you're dead." I always had an attitude. You should see that attitude change pretty quick. They rushed me to the hospital. The doctor told me: "Kid, if you keep doing this, you're going to die."

Several months later, another youth was also flirting with death. On a bitter cold October night Douglas and his friends were huddled in a doorway next to each other, trying to keep warm under a thin blanket. When the police suddenly arrived, everyone but Douglas ran. He was too drunk to move. The next thing he remembered was waking up in the police station:

> I had this long hair, and when I woke I saw this cop— she was a lady—standing over me, combing my hair. It nearly blew my mind. When she saw me open my eyes, she asked me if I needed anything. I said, "Yeah, some

pills." To this cop, right. She said, "No, you don't need that. How about some coffee instead?"

Bernie and Douglas were two of the several hundred teenagers whose drug addiction led them into the drug program at Covenant House. The program was started in 1987, as an increasing number of teenagers with serious drug problems were asking for shelter.

Young addicts enter the Covenant House program for a number of reasons. Many, like Bernie, begin to recognize the negative lives they led:

When I walked down the street, even in the nicest neighborhoods, where 95 percent of the people can be nice, I never noticed the nice people. The first people I'd meet would be the losers. The junkies. I never noticed people doing the right thing. I'd walk to the "cop" spot and I'd look at my friend and I'd say, "Bobby, we're crackheads." And he'd say, "Yeah, we are." And we just keep on walking to the spot. We knew what we were doing to ourselves. It was so insane. The scary thing is that I'd look at the whole thing and I'd say, "It wasn't that bad," but it was. It was as bad as it gets. I said, "You should be the man! you should be the man!" What made me the man was the same thing that made me the bum. Hanging out with drugs, making the scene made me the man, but it made me the homeless bum.

To overcome addiction, a person's values, moods, thinking and behavior must be changed. The therapeutic community socializes its members and forces them to look at their own behavior and that of others, and accept responsibility for their condition. Therapy teaches

Many young people who arrive at Covenant House have emotional and drug problems, which they are helped to overcome.

them to recognize their own feelings and become sensitive to the feelings of others. In the therapeutic environment, the goal is for drug addicts to become a family and learn to care for and support each other.

The drug therapy program at Covenant House is less intense than it is at many other drug rehabilitation programs such as Phoenix House and Daytop Village. Most residents at Covenant House are expected to complete the program in about eight months instead of two years, although some take more time and others less. The program is divided into four parts: Orientation, and Phases 1, 2, and 3. For the first seven days in the program, residents must remain on the floor twenty-four hours a day and attend group therapy sessions, Alcoholics and Narcotics Anonymous meetings, floor meetings and individual counseling. After the seven days, the residents are allowed to go outside for short periods of time as long as they are supervised by a counselor.

From the time a resident gets up at six thirty A.M. until lights out at ten thirty P.M., his day follows a set pattern: group therapy sessions in the morning; seminars in the afternoon on subjects such as spirituality, cultural diversity, health and sex education, HIV; and residence meetings in the evening followed by either Alcoholics Anonymous or Narcotics Anonymous meetings. The pattern is rounded out by afternoon sessions at the gym or walks.

As the resident shows progress, he graduates into increasingly higher phases. He is given more responsibility and privileges. He is allowed more visits, phone calls, an allowance and, toward the end of the program, is prepared to leave the residence and reenter society and transitional living.

Alberto, now nineteen, a former cocaine addict, remembers when drugs first entered his consciousness. "When I was in elementary school this teacher gave me drug education classes. 'This is pot,' she'd say, 'this is alcohol, this is cocaine, don't take this, it destroys your body, ruins your teeth and appearance.' Inside, I said, 'It won't

All Covenant House residents, including those in the drug program, have semi-private or sometimes private rooms. While the drug program emphasizes learning to live with others, it recognizes the need for privacy.

be me, it won't be me.' Then, about my second or third year of using drugs, when I really fell in love with them, I looked back on that experience. And here I am with some pot in my pocket. Do I care? No. I already had some stuff in my hand."

Alberto had started his road to drugs at nine. "When I was small I experimented with liquor and smoking. I felt that was really attractive. 'Hey, this is really good. Hey, I never had an experience like this. I'm going to try it again.' There comes a point where you can't stop. You say, 'I'm doing this because I like it.' You don't think about the bad effects it has on you, what it does to your body, your mind. It catches you off guard."

Alberto made the switch from acid, pot, and alcohol to cocaine:

I started because of the pain of my friend's death. I couldn't stand that pain. I needed something really strong to ease that pain. The drugs make you numb. It's not a matter of looking for new experiences. It's just a matter of blunting what happens day by day by drugs and alcohol.

Like many addicts trying to overcome their addiction, Alberto constantly acted out his anger in the beginning. He would scream at staff members and fellow residents and complain about everything:

I would say, "Hey, I haven't got enough food. I want a room change. Hey, I want to go out. I need to be with a girl. I need to have sex." Being on the streets, I adapted to that way of life, being a tough guy, using drugs. It was tremendously hard reversing that. It was painful, too. I was very good at pushing people away.

Alberto was fortunate to find support from several of the staff, particularly Queenie Rogers, who has over a decade of experience working at Covenant House. She was the type of counselor Father Ritter described when he wrote: "Without a mentor, somebody who can kick around inside a kid's head, talk to him about his attitude, why he does what he does, about how important it is to meet people halfway, a kid won't make it." Even in his worst moments, Alberto realized Queenie was "a tremendous help to me. She showed care, emotions, she helped me so much. She understood. I told her things I hadn't told nobody."

It wasn't easy. But Queenie wasn't intimidated by Alberto's anger. She was aware that he was beginning to verbally express the violence within him rather than physically express it, as he had on the streets. Behind his need to project a macho image to protect himself was a terrifying fear that lay underneath. Queenie did not push him. "When Alberto said, 'I don't need you people!' I told him that if you need us we are here. I saw that he was very angry. He did not know how to talk about what he felt. He did not know how to handle anger. He had a big problem with the word *no*." Alberto agrees with Queenie's assessment:

> **Time and again she had to lay down the law to me. The times I lost control, I would get physically upset, so mad, so sick of being on the floor, I would physically hurt myself, punch doors, shut down emotionally. If a staff member would see me doing something wrong, he would raise his voice and I would raise my voice and he would raise his voice higher, and I would try to go higher. It would go nowhere. A few times I threatened to leave, but Tony and Queenie talked me out of it. They made me realize that there's nothing out there for me. No money, no drugs. Finally I said to myself, These people are here to help me, not to hurt me. So why am I arguing with them?**

Alberto's rebellion was actually a good sign. Bruce Ritter, founder of Covenant House, explained in his book why those who act out have a better chance of making it:

> **The kids with fire in them, the kids still capable of passion and caring, these are the ones who can make it back if you can turn their anger around into positive energy.**

One of the key programs designed to help Alberto and all residents to overcome their addiction is group therapy. Every morning, the residents gather and, under the supervision of a trained staff member, talk about their deepest fears and pains. The residents

Covenant House offers a variety of therapeutic programs from counseling to individual and group therapy, depending upon the nature of the problem.

reveal to others the brutalities they have suffered in their lives and the degradation they have experienced as a result of their addiction. They also subject each other to frank and harsh criticism in an effort to try and change their behavior in positive ways. Most importantly, they begin to face the truth about themselves. Residents who honestly participate in this process gradually begin to give up their anger and face and accept the reality about themselves. Healing can begin. But few people can jump right in. It takes time and courage to truly begin.

At first, Alberto listened to others talk about their experiences and pain. He preferred to remain silent. But listening to people talk about their addiction gave him strength:

The more I was in group, the more I listened to these kids, the more I kind of identified with them. I said, hey, that's what I need to do, to talk about these things.

One Saturday morning, the group began to focus on Alberto. They were critical of his negativism, his bad attitude. One after another, they challenged him: "You really don't talk to people." "You don't cooperate. You're off in your own world." "What's going on with you? Talk about it. We haven't heard nothing about your past." "If you really want help, you have to talk about it to get better."

Slowly, with hesitation, Alberto began to talk about growing up in Brooklyn, trying to be a gangster:

It was painful. I knew I couldn't keep all that junk inside of me. My stomach started turning, my hands were getting sweaty and I'm thinking, hey I don't want to talk to these people. But they want to know something about me. I told them. I told them how I was physically abused as a child. I told them how sad I was at the murder of my best friend and what it was like to be homeless and an addict, ducking in alleyways, sleeping in hallways, in cars, parks. I started my day hustling, hustling for food, drugs. Lot of people sell clothing, watches, walkman players, sneakers, whatever will give you that extra ten dollars. You steal, sell other people's stuff, sell yourself, find any way to make money. Scrounge up what little money you can. It's like a job. You do your drugs, you do it over and over again, it continues and continues, . . . until you're really down and out where you really can't even move. You're sick, your bones are aching from walking or you're in jail. Anything could happen to you. You can

> **get murdered, get set on fire. There's a feeling, I don't care. What's the fear of dying?**

After Alberto began to reveal himself to his fellow residents, he was certain that none of them understood his suffering. He was surprised when other residents embraced him and said they identified with him and had experienced similar things when they lived on the streets.

Eventually, Alberto began to notice changes in himself. A big moment came during group therapy one day:

> **I confronted one of the guys. He got really mad and upset. He got up from his chair, which you're not supposed to do in group. He attempted to spit on me. In the past, I would have taken the offer to fight this guy. I thought it over. I knew if I fight this guy I'm going to get thrown out. I'll be back in the streets. I'm just going to swallow my pride and just take it. If I can take that, I knew I really wanted to get my life together. After that, I got better at taking other people's mess and turning it into something positive for myself.**

Alberto pulled himself up by his bootstraps and graduated from the program. He found a job and was placed in a special program offered by Covenant House called Rites of Passage. For two years, Alberto will live in a special residence while he works and prepares to live on his own. He is aware that addicts are never completely cured. At best, they are able to live without drugs, but there is always the danger of relapse. This is why Alberto plans to continue to keep in touch with support groups like Narcotics Anonymous to continually reinforce his recovery from addiction.

Some drug addicts who enter Covenant House seem so far gone that the fact that they can walk through the door is a minor miracle. Douglas, a former heroin addict who, as we saw in Chapter 1, lived on the streets of Los Angeles, presented the staff at Covenant House with one of their biggest challenges. Douglas had completely identified with the beat/hippie drug culture of the 1950s and 1960s, even though he was born almost twenty years later. He dressed like a hippie, talked like one, wrote poetry like the beat poets and wore his hair down the length of his back. He said he was willing to give up his addiction but made it clear to the staff that he was unwilling to change his lifestyle. As former director Steven Fox pointed out, "Douglas's lifestyle and drug problem were part of the same problem. He could not successfully give up one without giving up the other." The battle was on. Douglas recalls:

Most residents here complete orientation in thirty days. It took me eighty. I was acting out all over the place. I threw chairs. I got in fights. I threw plants across the room. I threw food. I dressed the way I wanted and not the way they wanted.

The moment of truth came in Douglas's third month in the program. He was still wearing his hair long as if it were the banner of his life-style. The staff gave him an ultimatum: get a haircut or get out. Douglas was at first defiant:

I decided to get out. To hell with them. They put the paper in front of me to sign, discharging me. I was thinking, Do I have enough money? I didn't. Where was I going to go? I didn't have enough money for a bus ticket anywhere. I knew that if I got back on the streets, I'd get high. I didn't want to do that.

Douglas told the counselor that he'd get a haircut but, as a last gesture of rebellion, insisted that Covenant House pay for it. They agreed. "After that, I began to change," Douglas says. "That was a turning point." But the change was not overnight. Still acting out, he remained in Phase 1 of the program for eight months, far longer than anyone else. "I was so embarrassed to be eight months and still in Phase 1. Everyone made fun of me. Phase 1 for life, they said." But like water wearing away a stone, therapy eventually wore down Douglas's pathology. It was a major triumph for him to graduate into Phase 2. For the first time in his life, he has begun to see himself as possibly leading a productive life without drugs.

The heart of the therapeutic program that has helped Alberto and Douglas is talking about feelings and facing reality about oneself. But for many, expressing their innermost feelings and fears is extremely difficult and painful. Sean, a recovered addict, recalls how painful it was for him to talk in group. Like Alberto and Douglas, Sean was acting out, smoking in his room, taking showers when he was supposed to be in bed, talking to girls on the floor below through the ventilator. But in group, he went through the motions, talked about things in a way that really didn't matter:

> In group, they said, "Get in touch with your feelings." I said, "I did so much coke, I didn't know what feelings are. I don't feel nothing." So I would talk about getting high. I played the system to do what I got to do and get out of here. But I didn't get real with myself until one day they had a closed house. Just group—no radio, no TV. Nothing, I broke down and cried [in one of the sessions]. It felt like a ton of bricks was off my shoulders. I told them how bad I felt when my ma brought me up from Texas when I was small. I never wanted to come up here. I cried because it hurt a lot

to come up here and leave all your friends. I feel if I didn't come up here I wouldn't be in the situation I am now.

In addition to group therapy, house meetings, seminars, and Alcoholics Anonymous and Narcotics Anonymous sessions are held to enable the recovering addict to verbally express his feelings, confront himself critically, make contact with reality, and change his behavior in positive directions.

Every night after dinner, residents hold a house meeting in which they publicly confess the good and bad feelings they have at that moment. The meeting is not as intense as a group therapy session and is designed to help air grievances, let off steam, and reinforce positive feelings. At one evening meeting, John expresses optimism about his future:

I have good feelings. I'm winning. This is the longest I've ever been clean in my life. I never succeeded in anything in my life, but if I pass this course, it'll be the first time I'll succeed.

Lionel remembers the happiest day of his past:

It was my tenth birthday. The whole family was at the beach—my cousins, uncles, everybody was sober. Everybody was chilling out. All the good things were happening.

When Raoul, playing the clown, says "I was happy when I was doing drugs," Gino corrects him: "You was never happy doing drugs." Raoul admits it: "It's true. I was happy *not* doin' drugs," he says.

Charles Matthews reads a poem he is writing:

Why should this soul live in despair/wanting to care?
This soul so cold/frightened to be bold
Frightened of rejection/but needing some connection
This soul so neurotic/courting a narcotic.
This soul filled with shame/with no one to blame.

Seated in the front of the room is Carlos. He has returned to the program after quitting several months earlier. This is his first night back. The residents welcome his return. Painfully thin, with a haunted, faraway look, Carlos is a heroin addict who, at that moment, is coming down from a high. The first time he was in the program, he lasted three months before quitting. The second time, two weeks. Now he is back for the third and last time. Tony, one of the counselors, leads the residents in a prayer for Carlos, emphasizing that this is his last chance to make good. "Lord, thank you for bringing Carlos back to us. He already has two strikes against him here. One more strike and he is out. Please, Lord, let him stay here until he is recovered." Tony is referring to the policy of Covenant House, which allows a resident three chances to complete the program.

Almost every resident at one time or another wants to quit. This becomes quite clear at the nightly Narcotics Anonymous meeting. Narcotics Anonymous or Alcoholics Anonymous (AA) hold alternate meetings every weekday evening at Covenant House. This evening's meeting is run by Tom, a barrel-chested, muscular ex-con, who combines compassion and toughness. Each person who speaks stands up, states his name, and confesses that he is an addict. He is then greeted by the group and is free to express what is on his mind. This evening, many of the residents talk about their desire to quit the program, a thought that is constantly on their minds. James, an alcoholic, begins to speak:

My mother died awhile ago. She died of AIDS. I think

about her a lot. Sometime I see her in my dreams and I wake up in a cold sweat. When she got sick I stopped seeing her. I promised I'd bring my daughter to see her and I didn't. I wish she was alive now.

James's face is filled with pain and anger as he continues. His voice begins to rise as he complains:

When I was drinking alcohol, I didn't have these feelings. I hate them. I can't make up my mind to leave or to stay. I'm here for the wrong reason. My wife gave me an ultimatum—stay sober. I think about alcohol. I think about the people I shot and when I was shot. I think about the times I've beaten my wife. I'm a woman beater. I feel I should be out there getting a job, supporting my family. My wife has trouble paying the rent. My kids need things. I don't know if some other man is in my bed. My wife says no but how do I know? I should be there. I'm jealous.

As James reveals the depth of his agony, every eye on the room is on him except one—Carlos's. He is slowly nodding off from the effect of the heroin in his body. Douglas tries to gently wake him before Tony sees him. Carlos opens his eyes, blinks several times, and sits up straight in his chair.

When James finishes, Tom responds to his seeming desire to get a job and support his family. Tom knows from experience that what James is really talking about is getting back on the streets and back into his alcohol and drug habit:

A job never kept me clean. This process will help you get through those feelings. But you have to go through the process to get past the feelings. When you drank

**alcohol you didn't have the feelings because you'd
knock yourself out. You'll grow through the feelings if
you let yourself grow. You have to think of yourself
first. Not your wife. Not your child. I can't say
whether or not you'll end up together. Maybe you will.
Maybe you won't. I don't know. You don't know. Only
your higher power knows what's in store for you.
When I was on drugs, it cost me my wife. I had to find
another wife and start all over again.**

As Tom speaks, Lionel excitedly raises his hand. Tom, smiling,
gives him the floor, saying that he's afraid that Lionel will explode if
he doesn't say what's on his mind:

**My name is Lionel. I'm an addict. I'm getting tired of
waiting. Every day, the rooms are getting smaller and
smaller. You have to wait for meals, wait to get out
with your supervisor, wait to go take a shower, wait
until someone opens the door to your room, wait to go
to the toilet. I haven't been with a woman since I've
been here and I love women. There are beaches out
there and I'm not there. I can't say I'm not going back
to drugs. I can't say I'd stay clean. But I think about
getting high in here more than I did on the street. I'm
just fed up with the waiting, man.**

Tom holds up a mirror of reality to Lionel by explaining what the
real world is like and how it is similar to the world inside this room:

**What makes you think that you're not going to wait
outside? When you go to a bank you're going to have
to wait on line and it's your money you're waiting for.
If you're driving a car, you're going to have to wait for**

the light to change if it's red. You're going to have to wait in line to buy groceries and wait for the elevator. Life is waiting, man. You have to develop tolerance and patience. That's what you're here for. You're going through a process. You can't expect to go from the first floor to the fifth floor without climbing the second, third, and fourth floor. Chill out, man. The beaches will still be there when you finish. They ain't going anywhere. You're not too ugly. You'll probably find a girl when you get out of here.

The group laughs and Lionel laughs with them. Only Carlos is silent. He begins to nod off again. Slowly, his eyelids lower until his eyes close. Douglas realizes it is hopeless to try and wake him. The next day, Carlos is gone. Two days later, the word is that Carlos has stabbed someone on the streets and is in jail.

Steven Fox, former director of the Covenant House drug program, has no illusions about how difficult it is for the residents to overcome their problems:

The road to recovery is hard and most of the residents yearn for the past while groping their way toward a drug-free future. I've seen kids who have been severely damaged who can change. The crucial point is when things start to get going good. That's when we see whether or not someone is ready to recover. Drugs has been the most mothering thing in their life. To walk away and give it up . . . that's hard.

Every day that a resident remains in the program is a small victory because the impulse to run away, to self-destruct, is always present. Bernie speaks for every recovering addict when he says:

Sometimes I wonder what I'm doing here. I think about the good times I had in Hollywood. All the girls. The drugs. The family that we formed. I thought I was it. I thought I was the man. I thought I was hip. Obviously I don't think about the bad times. It wasn't always peaches and cream. I'm not really facing my issues yet. If you want your car fixed, you take it to someone who knows how to fix it. If you want your life fixed, if you can't fix it yourself, you take it to somebody that knows how to fix it, that has fixed other lives. I am not having any luck with fixing my life so maybe it's time to shut up and listen.

What is the secret to recovery?

There is no secret. First and foremost is motivation on the part of the addict. Addicts must be willing to accept discipline, to work hard, and to realistically and honestly look at themselves. In turn, recovering addicts must live in a therapeutic community where they are supported by their peers and by a network of professional staff that cares for them and helps them believe in themselves. As Father Ritter wrote:

How can you help a kid to trust again, to take a chance, to believe in another person? Especially when he can't trust himself or believe in himself anymore. You love him. And if you really do that and you don't stop—and survive his testing and if you do love him, then a kid can begin to believe he really is okay, really worth it because nobody would love a piece of garbage.

4

WILD IN THE STREETS

Every day, Ben goes to work around ten o'clock in the morning. That's when the little old ladies whose purses he robs are usually coming home from the supermarkets with their arms filled with groceries. Ben has no conscience about what he does:

> If I'm walking down the street and I'm broke and I want some money and I'm hungry and if I see somebody walking—like a lady with a purse—I'm taking it. I don't care.

For Fast Eddie, a former drug addict and car thief, the day used to begin by searching for cars with keys left in the ignition. They were easier to steal. But even if the car lacked keys, it was no problem for Eddie:

> All I needed was thirteen or fourteen seconds and a screwdriver. With it, I would pop a door lock, open the door, pop the ignition and [be] off. Stealing cars was a high for me. The excitement of it was overwhelming, like a drug itself. . . . I would steal up to eight cars a day until I got one I really liked. Speed was everything—the faster, the more exciting.

Throughout the United States, millions of teenagers like Ben and Fast Eddie have been drawn into the criminal world, a life that can lead to sudden riches but more often leads to addiction, mental institutions, prison, and death. Most are children of single parents and have been born and raised in poverty. Some have mothers or relatives who lead straight lives but who, in their children's judgment, work for "chump change"—the street term for low-paying jobs or welfare. Others come from families that have been destroyed by drugs, alcohol, and disease.

Lacking job skills and education, and with few jobs available even for those who have work skills, many young people see no future for themselves in straight society. For them, the middle-class tradition of going to school, getting an education, finding a job, and raising a family has no relevance for their lives. As sixteen-year-old Freddy M. puts it:

> **School was corny. I was smart, I learned quick, but I was bored. I was just learning things when I could be out making money. I like guns, I like stealing cars, I like selling drugs and I like money. I'll be selling 'til I get my act together. I'm just a little kid. Nothing runs through my head. I'll know I need an education. If I get caught and do a couple of years, I'll come out and go back to school. But I don't have that in my head yet. I'll have a little fun while I'm out.**

For tens of thousands of teenagers, their only way of making it, in their view, is crime. Robbery and selling drugs will make them respectable in the eyes of their community and will provide them with the "good" things in life—designer clothes, fancy cars, expensive jewelry, and girls. In the bitter irony of the situation, many high school–age youths drive Mercedes, Jeeps, Cadillacs, and Volvos while their parents drive early model cars, walk, or ride the bus.

For many young people in our society, crime is a positive experience because it is more exciting, more glamorous, more meaningful, and more uplifting than any other experience they have ever known. It is an attempted escape from the hopelessness of their lives. As one expert noted, the life of poverty breeds its own destructive, often tragic consequences:

> **The underclass is a culture of despair, a ghetto culture where unmarried pregnancies are the norm, school dropouts and illiteracy the rule, . . . where pimps, drug lords, and gang leaders are successful role models. Social responsibility and work ethic is foreign. Money is something that comes in the mail—not something that has any relation to work.**

Many city teenagers involved in crime are involved with gangs. Some gangs are close knit and run like a military operation; others are loosely organized and formed for one specific activity, such as selling drugs or protecting one's turf. Gangs are a traditional part of American city life. Ever since the first immigrants settled in the slums of America's cities, gangs have flourished. In the nineteenth century, in New York, Chicago, and Boston, ethnic gangs—Irish, Italian, Jewish, and Chinese—played a major role in underworld life. In the mid–twentieth century, black and Hispanic gangs were formed. Then, as today, most gangs were composed mostly of teenagers and young men who stole, robbed, trafficked in illegal goods, fought other gangs, and murdered each other and sometimes their victims.

The values and the codes of gang life have remained basically the same from the nineteenth century to the present. Gang life has become far more violent, however. Claude Brown, author of *Manchild in the Promised Land*, wrote of how, in the 1950s, he was gradually drawn into the gang culture. Having been involved in a life of petty crime, he was now expected to become a full-fledged gang member:

> **I was growing up now. I would soon be expected to kill**

a nigger if he disrespected me. Like [my friends] Rock, Bubba Williams and Dewdrop. Everybody knew that they were killers. . . . I knew I had to keep up with these cats; if I didn't I would lose respect in the neighborhood. I knew I was going to have to get a gun sooner or later and that I was going to have to make my new rep and take my place with the bad niggers of the community. I remember Johnny saying the only thing in life a bad nigger was afraid of was living too long. . . . if you were hoping to be a bad nigger, you had to be ready to die. I wasn't ready to do any of that stuff. But I had to.

The peer pressure in gangs is enormous. One former gang member described it as follows:

A kid wants to be accepted so he will do what other kids are doing even if it's wrong. He does not want to be embarrassed or disrespectful by refusing to do something good or positive. The people I know would really disrespect you and sometimes hurt you if you didn't do what they wanted you to do. There's a code among friends, and if you say you want to be with them, then you'll do as they say.

In the 1950s, drugs were introduced into the ghetto on a large scale. Before then, drugs such as marijuana had been in the community for some time, but they had not made a serious impact on teenagers or gang life. That was about to change. Claude Brown recalled how heroin affected the community:

Heroin had just about taken over Harlem. It seemed to be a kind of plague. Every time I went uptown,

somebody else was strung out, somebody else was hooked. . . . Drugs were killing everybody off in one way or another. It had taken over the neighborhood, the entire community. I didn't know of one family in Harlem with three or more kids between the ages of fourteen and nineteen in which at least one of them wasn't on drugs.

At the same time that heroin addiction was raging in Harlem, another drug increased in popularity—cocaine. Cocaine had been around for a long time. In the 1920s, cocaine was used in tonics, wines, and teas, until people became aware it was addictive. Cocaine was even supposed to be used in Coca-Cola. In the 1960s and 1970s, people who used cocaine "snorted it," that is, took it into their bodies by sniffing it through the nostrils. Cocaine was also very expensive. It was very popular with the "in crowd," which included artists, musicians, celebrities, and businessmen. But it was too expensive for most teenagers.

In the 1980s, a major change took place in the economics of the cocaine trade. Production began to soar, especially in the South American countries of Bolivia, Peru, and Colombia. Between 1979 and 1989, the quantity of cocaine brought into the United States increased from 50 to 200 tons. The rise in quantity led to a dramatic drop in price, from $50,000 a kilo in 1980 to $12,000 in 1992. The quality also improved. A smaller amount had a greater impact.

The second major change was that people began to smoke cocaine in the form of crack. The cocaine was cooked (boiled in water), leaving a residue that eventually formed an off-white, hard mass. Pieces of this mass, called *base* or *freebase*, were chipped off and smoked, usually in a pipe. Users generally prepared their own freebase. Crack got its name because it makes a crackling sound when smoked.

Crack was a drug marketer's dream. It could be sold in small quantities for two to five dollars, which meant that poor people could afford it. Thus, a whole new, mass market was created for crack. Because it gave an intense high for a short duration, users kept coming back for more, often several times a day.

In the 1980s, drug selling became a major source of employment for unemployed young people and high school students both in and out of school. Gangs, called "posses" in some areas, took over much of the distribution of the drugs on the street, while the suppliers came mostly from the drug producing countries in South America, Asia, or the Mafia.

Today, most drug sellers in this country are teenagers. Drug dealing is probably the largest employer of youth in the United States. In New York City, some 150,000 teenagers are employed as runners, steerers, stash catchers, and spotters. Many drop out of school to work specifically in the drug trade. Teenagers are hired in the drug trade because laws were passed in many states sentencing drug dealers over eighteen to long prison terms. As a result, older drug dealers began to recruit youngsters like eleven-year-old Shawn. Shawn rode his bike in the streets like any kid his age. But he was delivering crack vials and messages for drug dealers:

I looked up to them. They had all that money. They wore the latest styles. They pay me between twenty and twenty-five dollars per trip. Sometimes, I'd make two or three [trips] during a day. I thought, I'm making me some money.

Fifteen-year-old Terry was earning fifty dollars a week folding takeout boxes at a restaurant in New Haven when one of his "honchos" came along and offered him a job that paid a thousand dollars a week. It was an offer, he says, he couldn't refuse:

We started hearing about cocaine, cocaine, cocaine.

**People started getting nice clothes. Girls started
wanting all kinds of crazy things—gold, leather, furs.
They'd be saying, "It's all about the dividend." I was
working but I couldn't find a job that would pay me
enough money. And there was always another guy who
was up. He'd have his nice outfit and he'd be saying,
"Yo man, you should get down, you should get down."**

Terry's job was that of a "work boy." He was stationed in a sec-
ond-floor hallway, where he sold small capsules of cocaine at ten dollars apiece to customers directed to him by the "piss boys," who
work on the streets. Piss boys are hired for their willingness to use
force or carry guns.

The work was dangerous. Customers might try and grab the
drugs and run. Boys from rival gangs might try to steal it. Undercover
police posing as customers to arrest the sellers were another danger.
But the money was worth the risk. On a good day, Terry sold three to
four hundred capsules of cocaine powder in ten-dollar capsules. For
working twelve hours a day, six days a week, Terry was paid a thousand dollars. With the money he bought suede loafers, black leather
shirts, a Rolex watch, gold caps to sheathe his teeth, and gifts for his
parents and girlfriends.

One teenage girl on the streets explained why young girls are
attracted to the dealers:

**Most of these girls out here ain't goin' anyplace and
they know it. But they like cars and going shopping,
just like anybody else. Girls want to be well-known,
like anybody else, and if they're not well-known themselves, they want to be with a guy who is well-known.
Drug dealers are well-known. They got the latest
styles. So if a guy asks a girl out for a date, a girl will
say, "What kind of a car you got?" And he better say**

BMW or Mercedes or Volvo. Because if he say, "I don't got no car" . . . she gonna say "What? The other brother, he takes me shopping in New York and you want to go for a walk?" A guy who's poor, he don't have no chance of getting a girlfriend here. That's why a lot of them become drug dealers and get down with the posses.

Many of these girls become addicted and pregnant. "Babies having babies" is a common and accurate description of the scene. Because many are unable to adequately care for their children, and because the fathers of the children have little interest in them, their children grow up wild and eventually turn to the streets and drug trade. Some girls, like Trisha, realize the consequences of their actions:

Having a kid is a big mistake, because when you're young like this, it stops you from going to school. . . . When we was younger, all we used to talk about was getting out of the projects. Now they're going to have to end having to stay here. All they'll be able to do is get on welfare and stay here the rest of their lives.

Some young people turn to drug dealing because they themselves are addicts. Sean, who eventually overcame his drug addiction at Covenant House, was a Texan who worked for Dominican drug dealers in New York to finance his habit. He stood on the streetcorner and steered customers to where they could buy drugs:

I'd sell a guy a dream and he would buy it. I'd target white people. I'd say, "I got the best coke around, trust me. I'm white too. Trust me. You're my own peo-

**ple." I was making a thousand dollars a week but I
smoked everything. Everything went for the pipe.**

The danger of an addict handling drugs is that he might begin to
tap into his supplier's cache. That's what happened to Sean. One day
he was given $15,000 worth of crack to hold. He smoked it up and
then left the area when the dealer put out a contract on his life.

The relation between drugs and gangs varies depending upon
the city. In the suburbs, middle-class teenagers, once considered
immune from gang life, are forming gangs in some communities and
using drugs, if not selling them. Some of these teenage gangs have
started fighting with each other on the streets and in shopping malls.
The weapons have escalated. "It went from punches to razors to bats
and now to guns," one teenager notes. "Last time a gang raided us,
they were wearing ski masks. Now it ain't nothing about fighting with
their hands."

In South Central Los Angeles, gang warfare has become a night-
mare, not only to the community, but to gang members themselves.
Joining a gang is the equivalent of growing up in a wealthy community and going to college. Everybody does it. Gangs dominate the
city's life. As former gang member Sanyika Shakur, aka Kody Scott,
noted in his book, *Monster*:

**Today, no school, library, institution, detention cen-
ter, or church is exempt from being touched in some
way by South Central. . . . The gangs in South Central
recruit more people than the four branches of the U.S.
armed forces do. Crack dealers employ more people
than AT&T, IBM, and Xerox combined. And South
Central is under more aerial surveillance than
Belfast, [Northern] Ireland.**

Los Angeles gangs are divided into two main groups: the Crips and the Bloods. Each group is composed of approximately fifty sub-groups called *sets*. Until a truce was signed after the 1992 Los Angeles riots, the Crips and Bloods had been mortal enemies. Fierce battles continue to take place between the sets. A set may be organized around a street, a project, or a neighborhood. It may have as few as twenty members or as many as 350. The sets often behave like a country at war, invading each other's territories, killing each other's citizens, and brutalizing each other's women. There is no mercy, as observed by Léon Bing in her book *Do or Die*:

Faro spots his enemy walking in his, Faro's, territory. Because his enemy is with his wife and infant child, he thinks he is safe. But Faro has other thoughts. He and

Members of the Bloods, a Los Angeles gang.

his "homies" climb into their car. Faro positions himself in the back seat and slides the AKG from its hiding place. He places it on his shoulder and slips the safety off. Slowly the car creeps up on his enemy until it is even with him. Faro cries out his gang's name and as his enemy turns toward him, horror in his eyes, Faro unloads the full clip in his automatic rifle into his body. His enemy lies on the ground, dead. His wife lies on the ground crippled for life, the baby still in her arms, bleeding from a wound in the foot. Faro is satisfied at his day's work.

The first loyalty of a gang member is to his set and neighborhood. One gang member described his feelings this way:

I don't feel connected to any other kids in this city, or in this country or in this world. I only feel comfortable in my hood. That's the only thing I'm connected to. That's my family. One big family.

In Los Angeles, joining a gang means total commitment. To devote your life to gang activities is called *banging*, or *gangbanging*. Sanyika Shakur explained what was expected of him once he was accepted into the Eight Tray Crips:

Banging ain't no part time thing. It's a full time career. It's bein' down when nobody else down with you. It's getting caught and not tellin'. Killin' and not carin', dying without fear. It's love for your set and hate for your enemy.

Once in the gang, the goal is to earn a reputation and command respect. The worst sin that anyone could commit against another was an act of disrespect. It does not even have to be intentional. Sanyika Shakur explains this aspect of gang life:

> **This is a world in which you can get killed for a small infraction like stepping on somebody else's shoes regardless of the condition of the shoes. The underlying factor that usually got you killed was the principle. The principle is respect, a linch pin critical to all people, but magnified by thirty in the ghettoes and slums of America.**

To earn respect, a gang member had to earn a reputation. G-Roc, a gang member interviewed by Léon Bing in her book *Do or Die*, told her:

> **[All] I'm trying to do is make a name for myself. I trying to have a bad rep. I got a little reputation but it ain't nearly where I want it to be. I want to fulfill my name. Be a straight criminal, be devious, do anything, be bad to the fullest. Anybody want to fight, we can fight. Anybody want to shoot, we can shoot. Want to kill, we can kill. Whatever. You know what I'm saying.**

Sanyika Shakur's goal was to reach the top of the gang hierarchy. Gang members are ranked like soldiers in the army from tinies and little homies to homies and O.G.s—Original Gangsters. Shakur was determined to become an Original Gangster. At the age of eleven, he killed his first man in a "mission"—a drive-by raid on a rival gang:

> **The seriousness of what I had done that evening did not dawn on me until I was alone at home that night. . . . I felt guilty and ashamed of myself. . . . I felt that they were too easy to kill. Why had they been out**

there? I tried every conceivable alibi . . . to justify my actions. There were none. I slept very little that night.

The guilt did not last long. For the next ten years, his life was centered around gang activities. Soon Shakur was a feared gunman. He killed often, mercilessly, and without compunction. Sometimes, he would drive by rivals, shooting them down as they stood in the streets. Other times, he would lay a trap for his victims. In turn, Shakur was tracked down by his opponents. Several times he was shot, critically wounded, and almost died. Once, his rivals tried to kill him while he lay in a hospital bed. Wherever he walked, whenever he sat in front of his television at home, bought a hamburger at a fast-food restaurant, took a drive, visited a friend, he never knew if he would suddenly feel a hail of bullets tear through his body and end his life:

I had no idea of peace and tranquillity . . . I've never been at peace and nothing has ever been stable. Motion has been my constant companion, from room to room, house to house, street to street, neighborhood to neighborhood, school to school, jail to jail, cell to cell—from one man-made hell to another. So I didn't care about living or dying. . . .

Living or dying—many young gang members do not care which one happens to them. Many of those who die are thirteen- to fifteen-year-olds, who, by the time their short lives end, are burned-out combat veterans. The fact that they are doomed to die does not disturb them. Greg, a former Baltimore gang member, says, "Parents ask their kids, do you want to live or die? The kids honestly answer: 'I don't know. We see death everyday around us. It's no big thing. We don't see another way of life.'"

Faro, who expects to die or spend his life in prison, expresses the despair that underlies the feelings of many gang members:

> **If you die, you die. Most gangbangers don't have nothing to live for anyway. . . . If they mother dead, they brother dead, they sister dead. What else they got to live for? . . . You see enough dying and then you be ready to die yourself, just so you don't have to see no more death.**

Greg says that many gang members do reflect on the meaninglessness of the gang wars:

> **There was no reason to them, no sense, yet they continue on and on day after day, night after night. Everybody on the street thinks about another life. Should I be doing this? But it's hard to believe in. It seems impossible. And you don't want to give the impression that you're weak.**

This despair combined with a fear of appearing weak is part of the reason that many gang members remain committed to the gangs even though they know their life is at a dead end. What sweetens their existence is the opportunity to make money in the drug trade and getting the better of their rivals. But there are other, deeper factors at work that lead young people into the life of gang warfare. A counselor at a youth facility in California told Léon Bing that the problem has its roots in family life:

> **The very fact that a kid is in a gang means that something is missing. So many of them are functioning illiterates. So many of them come from abusing backgrounds. The hardest cases were probably sexu-**

A female Bloods gang member showing the gang's hand sign.

ally molested or were routinely beaten. Probably both. . . . You find a gang member who comes from a complete nuclear family, a kid who has never been exposed to any kind of abuse, I'd like to meet him.

Some experts feel that by the time young people reach their teens, it is too late to effectively change their lives. They feel that too much effort has been placed on curing the individual rather than correcting the physical, social, economic, and educational conditions that will eventually push juveniles into delinquency. Yet, some gang members do manage to free themselves from the vicious circle they find themselves in. Shawn, who was a drug messenger at eleven and carried a gun at fourteen, had a mother who refused to surrender him to the streets even though his teachers, friends, and family thought he was destined for jail. His mother worked at three jobs to support them both:

I was worried I'd lose my son to the streets. But as long as I had breath in my body, I was going to fight for him. I wasn't just going to turn him loose. But I knew I couldn't raise him by myself.

It was a battle for his soul. His mother recruited her minister and Shawn's teacher to help her lead her son to better things. She understood his anger at his drug-addict father who abused her and abandoned them. Her dedication paid off. Today at seventeen, Shawn is an honor student, co-captain of his track team, youth leader in churches, and he plans to attend college.

Greg, who was shot in street fights, also gave up his gang way of life and is now in the process of overcoming his drug addiction. "What helped me was that I grew up with some values," he says. "My grandparents raised me and I went to church. I had something to build on."

Some change because they no longer are willing to accept the consequences. One teenager said:

> **I seen people hurt somebody bad and then they get hurt or worse. I'm young, but I be sitting there watching everything and I say, one day, everything catch up to you. Just watch. But then I say, "Who cares?" But the truth is, I ain't prepared to die. I ain't prepared to die.**

There is another dimension to the gang life that few people recognize—the fact that the gang reflects the world in which we live. Gang members see no difference between what they do and wars that nations inflict on each other. And what about the hate that many whites express toward blacks? Gang members say that what whites are seeing in gang behavior is the mirror image of themselves. As one gang member noted:

> **It don't matter what you say about gangbangin, . . . it don't matter if anybody understand it or not. We jus bringing home the hate. That's the kind of a world we live in.**

5

BEFORE THE JUDGE

When Cleon stopped by Michael's apartment on a spring evening, he asked Michael whether he wanted to get some money by making deliveries for a local Chinese restaurant or by stickups. They decided on stickups. Cleon had a toy gun in his pocket but Michael had a real one in his closet—a sawed-off .22 rifle.

About nine thirty P.M., Wilfred Noble, a tourist in New York, crossed the path of Cleon and Michael. Cleon was standing in a doorway wearing a red bandana over the lower part of his face. "Like Jesse James," Noble later recalled. As Wilfred started to pass by him, Cleon stepped in front of him and Michael moved in from behind. "Give me your wallet," Cleon said, "I've got a gun." As Cleon reached inside his coat to pull out the gun, Wilfred suddenly dashed into the middle of the street and began to yell for help. Michael says he began to laugh. "Come on, man, I'm going home," he told Cleon. "The dude's gonna call the cops!"

The police arrived quickly. Cleon and Michael were spotted on a subway platform and the chase began. Michael surrendered, but Cleon jumped onto the tracks and ran down the subway tunnel. At the next station, he dashed out the exit, carrying the gun in a bag. The police were close behind. Just before he was caught, Cleon tried to throw away the gun. But the police recovered it and found the bullet clip in his pocket.

In most states, juveniles like Cleon usually are tried in juvenile or family court, which, under a special set of laws, is designed for young people who are legally minors and considered juvenile delinquents. Depending on the state, a juvenile delinquent is someone who is older than seven (children under seven are generally considered incapable of committing a crime) and younger than sixteen, and who commits an act which would be considered a crime if committed by an adult. Because of the juvenile's age, he or she is not considered criminally responsible. In New York State, juvenile delinquency cases are tried in family court. Most of these cases involve teenagers under the age of sixteen who have been arrested for car theft, drug dealing or possession, shoplifting, vandalism, robbery, felony and assault. Sometimes, first offenders or those who commit nonviolent crimes are immediately placed on probation without ever having a trial.

Cleon's case was given to corporation counsel, the office responsible for prosecuting cases in family court. Victoria Butler, the prose-

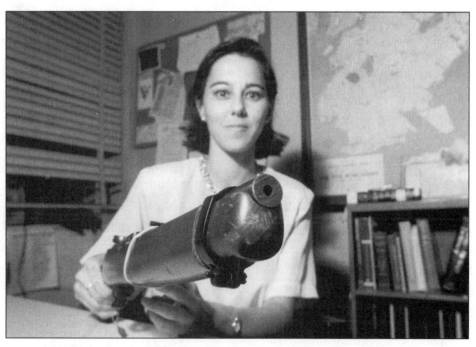

Victoria Butler, a prosecutor, holds the weapon used by a 13-year-old boy to commit a robbery.

cutor who was assigned Cleon's case, recalled, "When I looked at Cleon's folders, the first thing that struck me was 'Oh, my God. He's thirteen, with a gun!' " But despite his age, Cleon had crossed the line that Peter Reinharz, the chief corporation counsel for the City of New York, emphatically states "we cannot allow to be crossed. We will not allow violent crimes to go unpunished. Someone who sticks a gun in someone's face and asks for money is committing a serious crime."

Cleon was charged with attempted robbery 1, a Class C Felony, which in family court is a criminal offense, the C designating the degree of severity. The charge is moderately severe and carries a maximum penalty of eighteen months in juvenile prison. Had the victim handed over his wallet, Cleon could have been charged with a designated felony—a much more serious charge—and been sen-

Judge Judith Sheindlin of New York City's Family Court prepares to try a case involving a teenager accused of robbery.

tenced to as much as three years in jail. Cleon was fortunate that his victim ran instead of handing over his money.

Because Cleon was held in detention, he must either have a trial—which is called a "hearing" in family court—within three days or, if he is to be held longer, a preliminary hearing must be made to determine whether or not there is "probable cause" that the suspect is guilty. If the judge finds there is "probable cause," a date for the hearing is set. If the charges are not serious, juveniles are then usually released in the custody of their parents until the hearing.

On the day of his hearing, Cleon was brought in handcuffs from detention to family court, where he was held in a special room until the judge was ready to try his case. Cleon's case was one of thirty-seven cases on Judge Judith Sheindlin's calendar that day. Altogether, there are ten courtrooms in family court, which means that by the end of the day approximately three hundred cases will have been heard. Since no one knows what time any one case will be called, those summoned to court arrive early and prepare to wait. There is no guarantee that their case will be called that day. The judge waits until everyone involved in the case is present before a hearing is called. If someone fails to appear, the case is either rescheduled or dismissed.

The hundreds of men, women, and children who appear in family court every day wait for their case to be called in a large room outside their courtroom. A feeling of resignation and despair hangs over the room. Most people sit silently, some with their heads bowed. Mothers can be heard telling their children who will soon appear before a judge to "be polite," "tell the truth," "tell the judge you was only the lookout, that you didn't hit nobody." In addition to juvenile delinquency cases, the court will hear cases involving custody of children, court orders protecting a spouse from the threatened violence of another, visitation rights, and placement of children in foster homes and adoption. Almost every case involving the family is heard in family court. It is a sad scene that Judge Sheindlin says results from the poverty of the lives of those who appear in court:

> **What keeps us in business in family court . . . is a pervasive hopelessness. Most of the young people who we see believe that they're never going to have a kind of lifestyle where they have job opportunities, have a nice home, drive a nice car, take a vacation. There is a hopelessness that family court cannot do anything about. It comes from single-parent families that have a lot of kids, who . . . , even with the best of intentions, cannot care for all of them.**

Often, the lawyers for both the city and the juvenile accused of a crime will try to work out a compromise before the hearing in which the juvenile will plead guilty to a lesser charge. Judges are not bound by their agreement, but usually they accept it. The advantage for the teenager to plead guilty is that the punishment will be less severe than if a hearing had been held and he or she found guilty. The advantage for the court and the city is that it saves time and money, and cuts down on the paperwork.

Cleon has decided to have a hearing. Like most defendants who appear in family court, he will be represented by a court-appointed lawyer whose job it is to represent clients who cannot afford to hire a lawyer. The problem is that many of these lawyers are overworked and do not have time to study the case. Some are inexperienced. A few are incompetent.

Cleon passively sits in the court as witnesses begin to testify against him. Piece by piece, the case against Cleon is put together by Victoria Butler, the prosecutor. The victim relates how he was held up and identifies Cleon as the youth who said he had a rifle. Under cross-examination, the witness admits he never saw a rifle. The police officer who chased Cleon is able to tie him to the gun that was picked up by another officer who was at the scene. Cleon has no real defense and his attorney calls no witnesses to the stand. There is little doubt as to the outcome of the case. Judge Sheindlin finds Cleon guilty of attempted robbery. She orders a series of reports to determine his family situation, school record, psychological condition, and previous offenses. After she has studied those reports, Judge Sheindlin says she will decide what to do with this thirteen-year-old stickup teenager with a gun. Since the case is a serious one and Judge Sheindlin is concerned that Cleon might not appear, she orders him remanded, held in detention, despite the protest of his mother and lawyer.

It is understandable that many juveniles who are guilty want to beat the system and walk out free, but in family court this rarely happens. Most juveniles who are brought to court have been caught fairly soon after the crime. Since the consequences of going to trial and losing are always more severe than pleading guilty in the first place, the defense lawyer's job is to advise his client what the best course of action is. Some teenagers want a hearing even though there is little chance they will win. Others are poorly represented by lawyers who do not properly investigate their cases.

When Hector, sixteen, was charged with assault, a misdemeanor that rarely ends in incarceration, he decided to plead innocent. He was accused of being one of two men who assaulted a man and a woman on the street. Hector admitted that he was one of four passengers in a car into which a man threw hot coffee, hitting Hector in the face and chest. (The man later claimed the car almost struck him.) Two men from the car then got out and began to beat up the man and even struck his woman companion. Hector denies the charge that he was one of the two men, despite the testimony against him by one of the witnesses. The court must determine whether or not Hector is lying.

Usually cases like Hector's do not come to trial, especially when the accused juvenile does not have a record. Hector is doing well in school. He is about to enter the twelfth grade, although he admits to being absent more than he should. Hector does not want this case on his record. (Actually, records in family court are sealed.) Corporation Counsel Melanie Smith was willing to have Hector plead guilty to a lesser charge but she was unwilling to let him go completely free. "There was no excuse for what he did," she said. "A woman was assaulted and a man was beaten pretty badly. He will have to take some responsibility for it."

Unfortunately, Hector was ill-served by his defense attorney, who accepted Hector's version of the facts without seriously examining the case. He rejected corporation counsel's offer of a lesser plea, claiming that there was no hard evidence that his client was guilty. He asked that the case be dismissed. Since the two lawyers

Melanie Smith, the prosecuting attorney, presents her case to the court.

were unable to reach an agreement, a hearing was scheduled for Judge Sheldon Rand's court.

The first day of the hearing went badly for Hector. The woman who was assaulted took the stand and identified Hector as one of the two men who struck her and her friend. She says that she and her friend were crossing an intersection at which a car had stopped for a stop sign. The car suddenly moved forward as her friend was crossing in front of it and it almost struck him. He threw the contents of a coffee cup he was holding at the car. Two men then got out of the car and beat them up. "Hector was one of them," she says.

Her friend Paul, who was badly beaten and had to be taken to the hospital, gave the same testimony. Paul admitted to tossing coffee at the car because he was angry that the car had almost hit him. He did not intend to throw it at anyone. He also testified that as he was being beaten by the two assailants, he apologized for what he had done, but they continued to beat him. The hearing was then adjourned until the following day.

Now it is Hector's turn to present his defense. His cousin Raymond takes the witness stand and tells the court that he was the driver of the car when the incident happened. He states that his car never came close to striking anybody and that when the man threw hot coffee on Hector, the other two passengers in the car jumped out and beat them up. He says that Hector never left the car. He also tells the court that after the assault, he, Hector and another passenger waited for the police to arrive. They wanted to press charges against the man who had been beaten for throwing the coffee.

Raymond's testimony seems credible and the prosecuting attorney cannot shake it. For a moment it seems that the case is a stalemate. The cousin's testimony seemed to weigh equally against the victims. But at this point, Judge Rand, bothered by what he later said were "gaps" in the testimony, began to question Raymond, asking him to repeat in greater detail what he just explained. Raymond repeated the same facts without changing his story, confident that his testimony would be enough to acquit his cousin.

"And you're sure that Hector was in the car while all this was happening?" Judge Rand asked.

"Yes," said Raymond.

"Did you tell the police officer that?"

"What?"

"Did you tell the police officer that your cousin was seated in the car and had nothing to do with the assault?"

Raymond starts to hesitate. His confidence begins to slowly disappear. "No," he admits.

"Why not?" asks the judge. "Isn't it odd that you see your cousin arrested for a crime he didn't do and yet you don't even tell the police that he was with you in the car and not on the street?"

Raymond shrugged his shoulders. "I don't know. Everything was happening so fast. It was very confusing."

The judge dismisses Raymond, obviously annoyed. Hector's case is now on very shaky ground. His lawyer calls him to the stand. Hector's testimony will be critical to his own defense. His attorney questions him first. Hector repeats the same story that his cousin told: that he remained in the car, covered with coffee, while two other passengers jumped out and beat up the couple. "The coffee had gotten in my eyes and I couldn't see," he says. His testimony seems sincere. Melanie Smith, the prosecutor, then cross-examines him. "Why," she asks pointedly, "if you were seated in the car as you now claim, did you later tell the police that you were one of the two who beat up this couple?"

Hector's lawyer suddenly shoots up from his seat and objects. He is flustered and complains that he did not receive this information from the prosecution, but he is icily informed by the prosecutor that she did, in fact, pass the information on to him several days before the hearing. It is clear that Hector's attorney was unprepared and seems not to have studied the case thoroughly before the hearing. A police officer then takes the stand and testifies that Hector confessed to him that he was guilty. Both attorneys then sum up their case. Hector's lawyer says there is no evidence to convict his client. Corporation Counsel says that the evidence is overwhelming. The judge, quite angry, then orders Hector to stand. "It was quite clear based on the evidence that you did, in fact, assault both parties. I find you guilty of two counts of assault." Hector's mother breaks out in tears and cries out in court, "He didn't do it! He didn't do it!" The judge tells her to listen carefully to what he has to say for Hector's sake. He orders a series of reports to be conducted by the probation department, including psychological testing and placement. Hector is to make appointments with the probation department. He may remain with his mother as long as he keeps his appointments. The judge warns Hector that if he fails to appear for any of his scheduled appointments, the judge will issue a warrant for his arrest. The case is adjourned for several weeks when the judge, after reviewing the reports, will decide what to do with Hector.

Later, in his chambers, the judge says that he does not understand why Hector insisted on a hearing. "I ask myself, 'Did the lawyer do his job? Did he sit down with Hector and ask him what happened? If he really did the assault? And if he didn't, why did he tell the police that he did? Was he coerced into confessing? Why didn't his cousin tell the police Hector was innocent? And if he was guilty, why didn't he plead guilty to a lesser count—misdemeanor? If he had done so, I wouldn't have heard all the details of how badly the people were beaten. And most likely he would have received a lighter sentence." The judge shakes his head. He is angry that both Hector and his cousin perjured themselves and indicates that he might take action against them later on. He eventually decides to put Hector on probation.

It sometimes happens that in the middle of a hearing, a defense attorney will suddenly alert their client that the case is going badly and advise them to take a plea. Kathy O'Farrell, a Legal Aid defense lawyer representing a fifteen-year-old youth who stabbed another youth in a fight, aggressively argued her case, despite the fact that the prosecutor, Michelle Rowlins, had prepared a solid case against the youth. Ms. O'Farrell stated that her client, Michael, admitted stabbing another student with a twelve-inch butcher knife in the buttocks and leg, but claims he acted in self-defense. The student who was stabbed claims he had fallen down and was getting up when stabbed.

Ms. O'Farrell is quite belligerent in her defense and argues constantly with Judge Sheindlin, who rules her conduct unacceptable and reprimands her by entering her conduct in the record. The defense attorney requests time to take photographs of the site to prove her client acted in self-defense. The fact that she had not taken the photographs before the hearing annoys the judge. But wanting to give the defendant every chance to prove his innocence, the judge grants Ms. O'Farrell another date. However, the judge has her client locked up during the time. On the next day, Ms. O'Farrell is late, which delays the case still another day.

On the third day of trial, a police officer who witnessed the stabbing testifies that he clearly saw the respondent stab the student and that the student was unarmed and defenseless. After his testimony, Ms. O'Farrell holds a whispered conversation with her client and his mother. It has become painfully clear that despite the defense attorney's attempt to represent her client's wishes, the evidence against him is too strong. She recommends that he plead guilty to a lesser charge. He and his mother agree. Ms. O'Farrell then asks Judge Sheindlin to meet with her and the prosecutor in the judge's chambers. There, Ms. O'Farrell says that her client has agreed to plead guilty to a lesser charge of assault. Judge Sheindlin and Michelle Rowlins accept his plea, but, despite the efforts of his attorney, the judge refuses to release him to the custody of his mother. She orders him locked up to be sure that he will appear for sentencing.

Sometimes, a juvenile charged with a crime will fight a case, convinced that she is in the right even though the evidence is against

The prosecutor, Michelle Rowlins, and the defense attorney work out a plea bargain with the judge. The defendant has agreed to plead guilty to a lesser charge.

her. Samantha, who is fourteen, but looks eighteen, and is, in the words of one prosecutor, "a real tough street kid," insisted on a hearing after she was charged with helping to beat up a clerk in a grocery store. The clerk was so badly injured he was hospitalized for seventeen days. Four witnesses, including the injured man, testify against her. Each of them describe how Samantha, her mother, and sister came into the store and began to shoplift. When the owner told them to put the merchandise back and leave, they turned on him and went on a rampage in the store, striking the employees and overturning shelves and racks of food. Samantha managed to escape before the police arrived, but her mother and sister were caught. When Samantha went to the police station to see her mother, a policewoman told Samantha her mother was locked up and could not be seen at that time. Samantha cursed and struck the officer.

As witness after witness testifies against Samantha, she listens without visible reaction. When the moment arrives for her to present her defense, Samantha refuses to take the stand. Nor is there anyone else her lawyer could call to speak in her defense. The judge is puzzled. Why didn't Samantha save herself all of this grief by pleading guilty to a lesser charge? Her lawyer is as puzzled as the judge. "In her mind," he later speculated, "she might have felt justified for striking the clerk because her mother was in danger. It made no difference that she and her mother were wrong in the first place."

Judge Sheindlin finds Samantha guilty. But what to do with her? What can be done with a fourteen-year-old girl who, at this stage of her life, has shown herself to be a danger to herself and society, and yet is only fourteen. As she waited for reports on Samantha before making her decision, Judge Sheindlin reflected:

As a society, our primary responsibility is to protect ourselves. That does not mean that what is in the community's best interest is opposed to the respondent's. In making a decision about a child, I must ask myself, am I prepared to risk another victim? Have I sufficient confidence that this young person has understood from the experience in family court that this kind of conduct is not going to be accepted by the community in which he or she lives?

How do we protect ourselves from the Samanthas? When I say protect ourselves, I don't mean lock somebody up and forget about them. We have to take the Samanthas and get their attention. How do we get Samantha's attention? We don't say "Samantha, what you did was not a nice thing," because that's not going to get Samantha's attention.

Judge Sheindlin prepares to render a verdict.

Nor are we going to put her in an institution and forget about her. It's not the best thing for society, it's not the best thing for Samantha. We can say, "Samantha, we're going to take you and put you in an institution for the next eighteen months. We're going to try and give you some hope for the future. We're going to try and target in on what you can do, that's good, productive, and you can make a living [at]. If you don't get it in eighteen months, we're going to keep you there another eighteen months and try our best to make you get it, until you get it."

Before Judge Sheindlin hands down her decision, she will order an investigative report made on the teenager. This is standard procedure in family court. The report will contain a psychological analysis, family history, school reports and previous criminal record. The decision is handed down usually within one to two months after the trial. The judge has three options: supervision, treatment, or confinement. If the crime is a misdemeanor or first offense, the judge will most likely place the juvenile under the jurisdiction of the probation department with the warning that failure to obey the conditions of probation can lead to rearrest.

When the crime is more serious, the judge may also send the defendant to a residential facility, which may be unsecured or have limited security. Here teenagers eat and sleep, attend school, receive therapy, and are taught work skills. Depending upon the degree of restriction, they are allowed to leave the facility and visit their families. If they run away or leave without permission, they are returned to the jurisdiction of the court which may then place them in a secured facility or jail.

The toughest penalty a judge can impose is three years in prison for a designated felony—the most serious offense in juvenile court—or eighteen months in juvenile prison for other types of felonies.

Juveniles who have lengthy criminal records or who are involved in a homicide, but did not do the actual killing, are likely to receive stiffer sentences. Teenagers like Samantha, who are neglected by their parents or have previous records, are usually sent to facilities with limited security. Those like Hector, who commit a misdemeanor and whose crime is a first offense, are usually given probation.

Many reformers argue that jail makes juveniles worse and that the state should do what it can to save its young people from a criminal life—something they will learn in prison. Peter Reinharz, head of Corporation Counsel, strongly disagrees:

> **One of the great myths is send them to prison and they learn to get worse. Let me tell you something. If they want to learn to be tough guys, they can learn just as easily on the streets. Prison is not a college. Nor does anybody need to study hard to learn how to knock people down nor does anybody need to go to a mugging school. Maybe at one time, minor offenders were mixed with major offenders, but now everybody who goes to prison is bad news.**
>
> **I can't save kids. If you incarcerate somebody, if you put somebody in a program against their will, and they're just in a program because they have to go there, and you're telling them they have to change, what do you think the chances are that they'll change? Nil. The first person that's going to change somebody is that person. Some kids really see that they're going nowhere. Other kids don't even think about tomorrow or the day after or the week after. Some kids get better in spite of the system. Some kids get worse.**

For some juveniles, family court serves as a warning that they are headed for trouble. This is often sufficient to turn their lives around. For others, family court holds no fears. But as crimes committed by teenagers have become increasingly more violent, state legislatures, in response to public protests, have passed laws that permit teenagers to be tried and sentenced as adults. And many judges are taking as hard a line as the law will allow.

6

LAST CHANCE BEFORE JAIL

Ian was trying to appear cool but his heart was pounding in his body. Sweat trickled down his forehead as he stood before Judge Michael Corriero, waiting to hear whether or not the judge would send him to prison.

Ian was sixteen years old and in deep trouble. He had been part of a group of teenagers that had stolen candy and soda from a street vendor. When the vendor resisted, Ian and his friends severely beat him, kicking him as he lay helpless on the ground.

Ian was caught shortly after the incident and charged with robbery in the second degree and assault. According to the New York Penal State Code, second-degree robbery is considered a Class C violent felony and carries a minimum sentence of one and a half to four and a half years in prison. The assault charge carries an additional one to three years.

Ian's case was too serious to be handled in family court. Generally speaking, family court handles nonviolent crimes. Today, most states have special laws for juveniles who commit serious adult crimes, including murder, armed robbery, rape, and serious assault.

In New York state, teenagers fourteen or older who commit certain violent crimes are usually tried in criminal court. If a youth is thirteen and commits murder, he can also be tried in criminal court. When someone under thirteen commits murder, the maximum sentence they can receive is eighteen months. Under certain conditions they can be held in confinement until they are eighteen years old.

If a teenager is under sixteen and commits a violent crime, he or she is considered a "j.o."—a juvenile offender—and can be sent to prison. Teenagers over the age of sixteen are considered adults. Juvenile offenders usually receive lighter sentences than adults who commit the same crime.

Fortunately for Ian, judges in New York, as in many other states, have a certain amount of discretionary power. Under New York state law, a juvenile offender must go to jail unless the judge offers him youthful offender status, known as "y.o." If a judge feels that a young person is capable of benefiting from a special program, he may designate him or her as a "y.o." He may then assign the youth to a community-based supervisory program that may last up to a year.

While many judges, frustrated and angry at the increasing number of crimes committed by juveniles, are sentencing more juvenile offenders to jail, Judge Michael Corriero feels that to do so arbitrarily is often counterproductive:

> **It's not an idealistic approach to choose a rehabilitation program and probation. It's a more realistic approach to the problem. We can't put these kids away forever. The sentences are less than an adult. The most I can sentence most kids is three and one-third years. When the kid is eighteen, he's back in society. What does he come back as? A convicted felon? We have to pay attention to this, so that when these kids come back to society, they don't come back worse. My job is to protect the public. But how do I best do that? By putting a fourteen-year-old in jail for one to three to satisfy the DA [district attorney]? So the kid comes out at seventeen and now he can't get a job with a felony conviction. Have we really protected society?**

Judge Corriero's court, while technically part of the adult criminal court system, is especially designed to handle juvenile offender cases. While Judge Corriero presides over many different kinds of cases—murder, rape, assault, and armed robbery—most involve cases like Ian's, robbery and assault. Ian has pleaded guilty to the charge, and Judge Corriero, before he sentences Ian, asks him to tell the court exactly what he did. Ian explains that he "did not originally take the initiative" in robbing the vendor. He was fooling around, picking up soda cans, but when the vendor grabbed his arm, the situation got out of hand and turned into a robbery and assault. The judge expresses anger at Ian:

> **It seems to me that you are an unusually bright young man. You use words like *initiative*. Not many young people who appear before me even know what that means. Your record shows me that you do well in school. There's no reason for you to appear in this court. I am going to put you on probation and require you to attend a special program. They will give me a report on your progress. You will be on probation for the next five years. If you slip up, you can go to jail.**

Ian, relieved, says he understands and the judge dismisses him.

Throughout the day, there is a parade of teenagers before the judge. Many have participated in holdups and are being held in a detention facility because of the seriousness of their crimes. Fourteen-year-old Ernie is one of these cases. He claims that he was interviewing a man at three o'clock in the morning for his school paper when someone he didn't know came up and robbed the man at knifepoint. The victim claimed that Ernie was working with the youth that robbed him. Ernie's father has bailed him out of detention but the judge felt it would have been better to leave him there for awhile. Since he has been out, Ernie has been staying out late and disobeying his father. The judge makes it quite clear that if he continues to do this, he will lock him up until his trial begins. Ernie may be innocent as he claims—a jury will decide that. But in the meantime, he is under the supervision of the court. "I don't like to leave those kids unattended," the judge explains to Ernie's father. "I want Ernie to be on a curfew and to be home when he should. Otherwise I will put him in a place where I know where he will be at night."

Turning to Ernie, Judge Corriero asks him if he likes the detention center.

"No!" Ernie emphatically replies.

"Why not?" the judge asks.

" 'Cause bad people are there!"

"Then do what you have to do to stay out. I want you to have a curfew and listen to your father and do what he tells you. You have no choice in the matter. Do you understand?"

Judge Corriero is willing to go the extra mile on the juveniles' behalf because he knows that the defendants who come into his court are on the brink of going to prison. When a young man is brought before him charged with statutory rape, the judge speaks with the family of the victim before pronouncing sentence. When it turns out that the families of the victim and defendant are friendly, and there was some consensual sexual activity taking place before the rape was committed, the judge, with the consent of the victim's family, does not sentence the young man to a prison term. Since the defendant has been held in detention for several months, Judge Corriero considers that sufficient imprisonment. He places him on probation and sends him into a program with the warning not to see the girl or to get into any further trouble.

Judge Corriero is sympathetic to some of the problems young people on trial have, especially when it involves testifying against others. One fourteen-year-old has pleaded guilty to arson and it is clear that he was an accomplice but not the main actor in the case. The district attorney wants the fourteen-year-old to testify against the person who actually set the fire as a condition of probation but Judge Corriero refuses to go along. As he explains:

> **Very often when dealing with young people who have strong attachments to a group, you have to take that into account. I agree that everyone has an obligation to cooperate. But when you are dealing with kids who are members of groups, asking them to not only admit their own guilt but implicate others, it adds a dimension that might not be warranted. A young person might be prepared to admit his own guilt but not to rat on his friends. If someone is willing to plead guilty, I'm willing not to press charges. You have to leave someone with a little self-respect to straighten themselves out.**

Most of the young people who end up on probation have committed nonviolent crimes. Many have been on the streets since the age of nine, carrying guns for self-protection, and exposed to drugs and alcohol. Many of their parents have served time. They have seen family members killed, sometimes in front of their eyes. Most youth have family problems. The probation officers try to help them and their families straighten out their lives.

Throughout the United States, almost every community is seeking to find a way to help troubled young people straighten out their lives without going to prison. A large number of youth crime prevention programs have been set up from home supervision and community-based programs to group and foster homes. If possible, the courts and probation departments like to keep young people at home if the family is stable and the environment is not too destructive.

In Maryland, the Choice Program is one that works with children at home. The program offers young people in trouble tutoring and sometimes psychiatric counseling and job training. The case workers who supervise the young people are on call twenty-four hours a day. They visit them three to five times a day, seven days a week, for three to six months. They spend time with them in school, at home, and on the streets.

In most states, youthful offenders who commit nonviolent crimes are often assigned probation officers before a hearing is held. Persons who commit violent crimes may also be given one last chance. Probation can last from six months to two years, depending on the crime. At least once a week and sometimes twice a week, juveniles meet with their probation officers. Probation officers encourage youthful offenders to talk over their problems and find constructive solutions to their lives. Impulsive behavior is a big problem for many. Takeeshe, a sixteen-year-old who hit another girl with a brick—"because we didn't like each other"—believes fighting is the answer. Her probation officer is trying to get Takeeshe to think before she strikes out.

Some youthful offenders treat probation as a joke. Often the joke is on them. When sixteen-year-old Montel failed to show up for school, the school notified his probation officer, who immediately searched for him. Her first stop was the apartment Montel shared with his grandmother. She was there but didn't know where Montel was. She said that the reason Montel was not in school was because he didn't have the carfare. The probation officer then questioned the grandmother and soon discovered that she had just lent some money to a woman in the building who stashed guns for Montel and a couple of his friends.

The probation officer checked the apartment and saw two bottles of wine cooler in his room. Her instincts told her that Montel was back in the life again. As she left the building, she spotted Montel with his friends. He was wearing a new coat that he couldn't possibly afford unless he was involved in criminal activity with his gang. If so, she would send him to a juvenile detention center.

Some youth crime prevention programs focus on keeping the family together when a youth gets in trouble. One family preservationist reports:

> **Kids don't exist outside families. Whenever the kid has a crisis, you can assume the family has a crisis. We saw parents who did not have control over their kids; we saw parents who did not have parenting skills. We saw families overwhelmed by economic pressures. I was really tired of the fact that I was seeing children who said that if I had someone working with them, they wouldn't be here [on probation]. I vowed we would focus on the family and prevent children from coming in.**

Family preservationists work with troubled families for up to eight weeks. The counselors help solve a number of problems from teaching young people job skills to finding housing for the family.

Schools also offer programs to help youths in trouble. These include alternative education programs for students who have been disruptive in class or absent from school. The students often come from poor and middle-class families, from farms and inner-city neighborhoods. Sometimes they have learning disabilities or family problems. Some are addicted to drugs and alcohol. Some are runaways. Almost all are considered "misfits and losers" by those who know them, and most of them would not disagree.

In Poughkeepsie, New York, the corridors and classrooms of one alternative school are filled with tension, cursing, confrontation, and backtalk. But in the small classes there is also a lot of caring and attention from teachers who are supported by social workers who offer counseling and support for parents. Some students, like eighth-grader Rollie Williams, find the school peaceful, despite its seeming chaos. In his other school, he was suspended several times for fighting. "I didn't like school," he said. "I didn't even want to go." But he was surprised to find the classes small in the alternative school and the teachers responsive. "I ask for help now and the teachers come right to you."

Many kids still see school as a prison in which they are the prisoners. They regard all adults as enemies who cannot be trusted. Ruth Klein, principal of the Poughkeepsie alternative school, understands this. Her philosophy is to convince students that "there are people in society who can be trusted. If I tell you something, I will do it. You don't have to love me but you can trust me."

One program that Judge Corriero favors is the Youth Advocacy Project, a program designed to reach young people on the verge of going to prison for adult crimes. "What Youth Advocacy does," explains Charmane Wong, its director, "is that we go into the detention center and interview juveniles under sixteen who are awaiting trial. We try to select those kids whom we think have a good chance of making it on the outside if they get some guidance. We then recommend to the court that they be placed with us. If the court agrees, sentencing is postponed until we work with the juvenile awhile. We then set up a program for him which we monitor. He must go to school, obey a curfew, meet with his counselor, and stay out of trouble. After a few months, if we feel that he is doing what he's supposed to be doing, we tell the judge. The judge will then usually put him on probation. He'll be sentenced, but the sentence will be suspended. However, if he messes up, he'll be sent to jail to serve out his time. Many judges warn the juveniles that if they fail, he will give them the maximum under the law."

The Youth Advocacy Project most often deals with juveniles whose problems at home are enormous. One young man in the program lived in a car, another's mother turned up dead in a garbage bag, three had mothers killed by their fathers. Twenty percent of the young people in the program have a parent behind bars. Forty-five percent have at least one parent who was a substance abuser and sixty percent come from single-parent homes.

How effective are programs like Youth Advocacy? Over 90 percent of the juveniles it supervises have successfully completed its program. But there are failures. Gary is one of them. Rafael Ortiz, a case manager at the Youth Advocacy Project, first met Gary when he was fourteen and in the Spofford Detention Center for robbing and slashing a student.

"When I first saw him, Gary was a small kid," Rafael remembers. "He was polite, charming and smart. I looked at his record and I saw he had been in family court, but I thought maybe we could break his pattern of getting in trouble."

Gary acknowledges that his life was on the edge. It was not the first time he had been in a detention center. When he was thirteen, he was arrested for firing a gun at another student. He blamed his troubles on his friend. It was not the first or the last time he would claim that a friend got him in trouble.

> **I had never used a gun before. I didn't know how it worked. But my friend, he had this gun in his bag, and when I saw this guy who I had some trouble with, my friend handed me the gun and said, "use it." I told him I didn't know how. He said "Point it and pull the trigger." So I did. Just like on TV.**

Gary missed. He spent the night riding around on the subway and was finally arrested when he returned home. He was sent away to a residential facility. Several months later, he was back in detention. He was accused of stabbing and robbing a student at another school. Gary denied it but there were witnesses who testified against him. It was at this point that a counselor at the Youth Advocacy Project discovered Gary and decided to invite him to join the program. Gary remembers that it was like an answer to his prayer:

> **I was in detention center with my friend and we were both facing time. Then "God got me." I found religion in the chapel there. So did my friend. I was crying and hugging everybody. I was never going to get into trouble again.**

The judge agreed to let Gary enter the program. Gary remembered saying, "Thank you, Jesus," as he left the courtroom. Rafael began to work with him. He got Gary into a school. He had long talks with him. Gary seemed to be responding. Every day, he would show up at the Youth Advocacy Project offices and learn how to use a computer. He attended school on a regular basis. But "incidents" kept cropping up. A friend of Gary's was shot and killed. Gary himself was shot in the arm. He said it happened when somebody held him up for his coat and he ran. Rafael later discovered that Gary had money to spend, enough to pay someone $700 for a phony driver's license. Gary was accused of firing shots near a school, but charges were never pressed. Rafael recalls his response to Gary's new set of problems:

> **I believed Gary at the time when he said he was innocent. The judge was willing to give him the benefit of the doubt. When we went back to court and I reported that Gary was doing well in the program, the judge gave him one to three years for the assault and one to three years for the robbery. Then he put Gary on probation. He said that if he didn't get in trouble and did well in the program, he would remain free. But if he got in trouble again, the judge made it clear that Gary would receive the maximum sentence of each count. He would have to serve six years in jail on the old**

charges plus whatever time he received on any new charges.

In July of 1993, one year after Gary entered the Youth Advocacy Project, he was graduated from the program. Rafael was pleased with his progress and told Gary that he had the chance now to get his life on track. Three weeks later, Rafael learned that Gary was back in Spofford. He had been arrested for his involvement in the armed robbery of a store. Once again, Gary claims that friends got him in trouble. He says he gave them a lift in a borrowed car (which he was driving with an illegal license) to buy some sneakers. When they got inside the store, his friends pulled out guns and held the store up. Gary says he ran and drove away. His friends were arrested in the store. Gary was later identified as part of the gang.

Gary now faces a minimum of eight years in jail if he is convicted of the robbery. He will have a jury trial and it is up to twelve men and women to decide if they believe Gary's claim of innocence. Rafael sums it up this way:

We tried to do everything we could for him, everything that was possible. We put him in special programs, gave him a special education, talked to him, warned him, but he thought he could fool everybody. He only fooled himself. If he goes to jail for eight years, we've lost him. Unless some miracle happens, he'll come out a criminal.

Can juveniles like Gary be saved? Only if they want to. Judge Corriero thinks it's unrealistic to expect the courts to succeed where the family has failed:

The vast majority of these kids have problems that are very difficult to deal with. It takes thirteen or

fourteen years for them to get here. It's very unrealistic to think that a couple of minutes with me is going to change anyone. I like to think that every kid has the capacity to change. But often the problems are deeply emotional and psychological. Many of these kids have been in foster care since birth. We need to get these kids early, when they are three and four years old and get them into programs then.

Judge Corriero often sees elements of hope in some of the teenagers he has tried to help. He remembers the case of a fourteen-year-old mugger with a record. The judge was reluctant to grant him youthful offender status because of his previous record. Yet without that designation the youth's record could not be sealed (never made public). The judge then asked the young defendant why it was important to him to have his record sealed. The youth looked at the judge and answered without hesitation: "Because when I get out of jail, I would be brand new."

7

SHOCK INCARCERATION

When Dennis Tal was sentenced to five years in prison in South Carolina, he was stunned. "I broke down in the courtroom and cried," he said. Dennis had been riding in his brother's car when suddenly the police began chasing them. Dennis's brother tried to get away. Before their car crashed, his brother had run five police officers off the road, sending four of them to the hospital. "I'll never forget lawmen throwing me down on the road and sticking a shot gun in my back and alongside my head," Dennis said.

At first, the state of South Carolina was set to throw the book at Dennis for drug dealing and injuring the police officers. He was facing more than twenty years in prison. But Dennis was able to convince them that he did not know his brother was a drug dealer, and was, in fact, carrying drugs in his car. He told the prosecuting attorney that he was unable to stop his brother from trying to escape the police. The state's attorneys agreed to throw out all the charges but one—distribution of a controlled substance. Under that charge, Dennis could still go to jail for five years, but the prosecutors said that if he pleaded guilty, they would recommend to the judge that he be sentenced to the time he had already served in jail awaiting trial. Dennis, although he felt that he was innocent, agreed. The consequences of going to trial and being convicted were too great a risk for him to take.

The judge did not accept the prosecution's recommendation. He felt that Dennis should have tried to escape from the car. Because he did not, Dennis would have to accept some of the responsibility for the injury of the police officers. "I was too scared to get out of the car," Dennis told the judge. Even though Dennis was a family man with a steady job and a home with a mortgage, despite his lack of a criminal record, the judge sentenced him to five years in jail.

"It hurt me, hurt me bad," Dennis said. "It meant my job was going to be gone, my home was going to be gone. My family was going to have to suffer. I was fixing to lose everything I ever worked for." But just before he was to be transferred to prison, the state of South Carolina offered him an alternative program. It was called Shock Incarceration, a program that was offered to nonviolent first offenders. In many states, the program is called *boot camp.*

Boot camps have been offered as an alternative to prison since the early 1980s. Basically, they are special facilities in which first offenders undergo intense military training similar to that given to new recruits in the Army and Marines. Depending on the camp, the program lasts from three to six months. The philosophy behind boot camp is that military training will give discipline and structure to young people whose lives are undisciplined.

In South Carolina, only first-time offenders between the ages of seventeen and twenty-nine whose crimes are nonviolent and whose sentences are less than eight years are eligible. All candidates must first pass a physical and mental test. The program consists of ninety days of intense physical and disciplinary training, education, and manual labor. After ninety days, the offender is freed on parole. Without the program, most offenders would have to serve between one to two years in prison before being eligible for parole. It is not surprising that almost every offender offered the shock training of boot camp takes advantage of it.

For young men like Dennis Tal, Shock Incarceration was a godsend. "I was looking at spending at least eighteen months in jail," Dennis says. "Now I knew I could be out in ninety days. That meant I could save my job and my house as long as I could complete the course."

Dennis was sent to the Shock Incarceration unit in Rembert, South Carolina. The unit is physically a part of the Wateree River Correctional Institution, a minimum-security prison. The Shock unit is separate from the prison and there is no interaction between the residents of the two institutions. To young offenders, however, the grim faces and tattooed bodies of the inmates of the correctional institution serve as a constant reminder of what awaits them if they fail the Shock program.

The offenders arrive in groups of thirty-two men. They will live, work, eat, drill, and play together as a group until they graduate. "Life in Shock," Deputy Warden Howard Arden explains, "is that of a mili-

The Shock Incarceration or "Boot Camp" unit at Wateree River Correctional Institution. Deputy Warden Howard Arden stands in front of two of the inmates.

tary boot camp. We organize the inmates into platoons like the Army. Each platoon comes in as a group and they graduate as a group. They work together, study together, and live together. It builds morale and *esprit de corps*."

Upon arrival, each man is given a military haircut, down to the scalp. He receives a uniform and is assigned to one of two barracks, each of which holds three platoons. New inmates are instructed in the rules of the institution and the punishments for violations. The main thing each man must learn is that everyone needs permission for almost everything he does. No one can talk, move, go to the bathroom, sit down and eat, or carry out almost any activity without first asking an officer. As one officer explains to a new group of inmates: "Rule number eleven is simple. Just keep your mouth shut. You are not allowed to say anything until I give you permission." Violations of the rules are punished by extra physical training. If a violation is serious, the inmate is set back two weeks, which means he must remain at the camp 104 days instead of 90. A second violation can lead to another two-week setback. Any violation after that, no matter how minor, means dismissal from the program.

The day in Shock begins at five A.M. The inmates wash, shave, and make their beds. At five thirty, platoons line up for one hour of intense calisthenics and running. The eventual goal for each man is to be able to do one hundred sit-ups in two minutes, one hundred push-ups in two minutes, and run two miles in fourteen minutes before leaving. Warden Arden says the joke among the officers at Shock Incarceration is, "If we can't get these young offenders to go straight when they get out, at least they'll be able to run so damn fast, law enforcement won't be able to catch them."

Between six thirty and seven A.M., the men are back in the dorm for inspection of their living quarters. Breakfast is from seven to seven thirty. After breakfast, the platoon will work until three thirty P.M., with a half-hour break for lunch. Some platoons work on the prison farm, others go off the grounds and work on highways and

The day's routine at Shock begins with exercise. Wakeup is at five A.M.

public buildings. Men clear roads, cut trees, construct buildings, and clear brush. All the jobs involve hard manual labor, which teaches them work skills at the same time. If they need to speak or go to the bathroom they must raise their hand for permission. When there is a natural disaster in the area, like a hurricane, Shock inmates will clean up debris and repair damaged buildings.

At three thirty P.M., the inmates attend school until dinnertime. Many of the young men are high school dropouts. They are encouraged to work for a G.E.D. Counseling is also offered to help men learn basic life skills that some of them have failed to acquire, such as how to control their anger. At six thirty P.M., the platoons eat dinner. From seven to eight, they go to study hall, where they do homework. From eight to nine, they have free time. From nine to ten they shine their shoes and prepare for inspection the next day. There is no television or radio during the week. No food is allowed in the barracks and smoking is forbidden. Lights are turned out at ten P.M. Until bedtime, no one is allowed to sit, lie, or rest on their beds. If anyone has extra duty, he must do it ten o'clock to midnight, which means he will have only five hours to sleep that night.

On weekends, there is no work, but every man receives two hours of physical training and two hours of drug lectures. Inmates play sports, watch television, or after the first month, may receive visits from their parents, grandparents, wives, and children. No other family members or any friends are allowed. Each inmate may make one five-minute phone call a week and is allowed to carry only ten dollars to spend in the canteen. Visits, television viewing, visits to the

Discipline at Shock is based on military training.

canteen, and phone calls are considered privileges and can be taken away. Shock residents are not allowed to smoke but Dennis says, "some people don't get the rule through their heads." Some try to smuggle in cigarettes and if they get caught, they receive more physical training and can even be set back two weeks. Fighting is also forbidden, although fights do break out, especially when someone tries to establish a reputation for himself. But there is none of the violence in Shock that one finds in regular prisons.

What does this rigorous training at Shock accomplish? According to Deputy Warden Howard Arden, who spent twenty-four years in the army before heading the Shock program, the answer is discipline:

> **The whole thing is that we're trying to show these young men that they could do the right thing and enjoy their life. We're trying to put some discipline in their lives because they never had any discipline before. Without discipline you're unable to be a good student, a good athlete, a good spouse, a good parent, and above all, a good Christian.**

Many young men who come into Shock were leading productive if undisciplined lives on the outside. Tim Anthony had a successful career as a salesman when he received a four-year sentence for drug trafficking:

> **I had a good job. I don't smoke, don't drink, came from a good religious family. I was making money and I had an opportunity to make some more money and that's what got me. It's called greed.**

For Tim, the experience of Shock Incarceration has been a difficult one, as he explains:

It's hard now. As it progresses, it doesn't get any easier. You just adjust to it. From the first month that you're here, it's a mind trip. They try to break you.... [They try] to find out what you're like, what kind of attitude you have, if you got self-discipline. The rules are so easy to break.

Officers try to push the inmates to their limit. "They're like a pack of dogs," one officer commented about the resistance he encounters at the beginning. "Dogs that try to rip at you." Troy Blackwell, an inmate, sees Shock as a mind game. "If you can stand

Hard labor is an essential part of the program at the Shock Unit. Inmates work from eight A.M. to three thirty P.M. with a half hour for lunch.

the stress, you can stand anything." When one inmate began to cry because he was afraid that his girlfriend would not wait for him, he received no sympathy from the officers. One told him, "Wipe off your tears and act like a man."

For Anthony Lester, who was sentenced to five years for receiving stolen goods while on probation, accepting discipline was the toughest test:

> **The hard part was taking orders. I had a quick temper. The first month it was hard to put up with the officers. People say something, I'd argue with them. But the officers sat down and talked to me. They'd teach me how to get along better. I put it in my head. I would try to do the right thing. It surprises me that I stuck it out but now I'm going to graduate.**

To Dennis Tal, the program has been easy because he was able to accept the rules without any problems:

> **If you do what you're told, you can breeze right through this thing. It makes your mind stronger. Shock is candy compared to being in prison. If you want the easy way out, come to Shock, 'cause Shock is the easy way out.**

Some, like Lonnie Thomas, so enjoy the program that he recommends it to all young people, whether they're in trouble or not:

> **There's nothing hard about it. All you got to do is do what you're told and stay out of the officer's face. It's a good place to be. If I had another chance to come back I'd come back.**

On the surface, Randy Medelin, who was arrested for auto theft and sentenced to serve seven months, seems to benefit from the program. Somewhat smaller and weaker than many of the young men in Shock, Randy is aware of what could happen to him if he went to prison. "I know I wouldn't make it in the yard. Because of my size I'd get beaten up or shanked," he says. When Randy arrived at Shock, he was scared:

The officers were on my case. It got easier as I learned what the rules are. I never had any discipline. I don't get along too well with my stepmother and father. Here I'm learning some discipline and self-respect.

But Randy is struggling in the program. He has been set back twice and is on the verge of getting kicked out for continual violation of the rules. He claims that the reason he gets into trouble is that others take advantage of his size to set him up. But others say that he is primarily responsible for the trouble he finds himself in. If Randy fails the program, he will be sent to prison and will not receive any credit for the time he has served in the Shock program. He vows that he will finish and graduate:

The program taught me that the best thing in life is life itself. Life is too short, there's too much to see and do. Prison isn't a life I want to be a part of. When I get outta here, I'm gonna be an angel. I'm going to be the sweetest angel you ever saw.

How successful is Shock Incarceration? Warden Arden states with pride that over 90 percent who start the program finish it and only 11 percent of those who graduate are arrested again. Is ninety

All inmates are required to study. Those who have not finished high school are encouraged to work for their G.E.D.

Shock offers inmates counseling on such life skills as learning how to control anger and dealing with authority figures.

Inmates who disobey the rules are disciplined by officers and may also have to spend additional time at the unit.

days enough to do the job? Warden Arden thinks so:

> **I think ninety days is enough. In the military or college, anyplace . . . where they put stress on you, after ninety days there is a break so you can back up and regroup. I don't think those programs that last for six months accomplish a great deal.**

One young man who, after Shock, went on to college, graduated and started what is today a very successful business testified in a letter to Warden Arden what Shock Incarceration can do:

> **Most of you probably don't remember who I am. I was**

SPU 148008 and a member of the very first group of screw-ups. I was the tall redhead that broke into cars. My crimes were too severe for probation, but locking me up for five years was questionable. If the judge did not have Shock probation as an alternative, I would either steal, be in jail, or not alive. Without you all, at Shock Probation, I would not have anything I have today. No family, no degree, no possessions, nothing. My life was spiraling downward and you caught me and kept me from falling through the cracks. . . . Thanks again for all you have given me.

Dennis Tal, who was recently released and has returned to his family and job, confirms what others have said about Shock Incarceration:

I guarantee you by the time people are ready to leave here, they'll have a little bit of self-respect. They'll have enough self-respect that they're not going to come back to prison. Most of them know what it's like in the prison next door. Nobody wants to come back here again.

8

PRISON

Despite the programs designed to get young people back on track, there are thousands of teens who will end up in prison, some of them for life. In the 1960s, it was relatively rare for a teenager to be sent to prison, even if he committed a violent crime. "In those days, you knew if you did something serious, you'd go to a juvenile joint for a few years and be back out on the streets again," Jim Anders, who is serving a life sentence at East Jersey State Prison, recalls. "It was no big deal, unless you did a crime that was pretty heavy and got a lot of publicity." In the 1970s, the courts began to impose heavier sentences on teenagers. Today, the United States has the highest incarceration rate in the industrialized world. Out of the approximately 1 million men and women held in prisons, almost 70,000 are teenagers. Another 750,000 juveniles reside in public and private facilities.

Once, going to prison was a source of shame and sorrow in a community. When a youth went to jail, it was spoken about in whispers. Now, in many communities, prison has become a rite of passage for many youths. One young man said, "Going to prison is like going into the army. You go for a couple of years, do your service and get out." Younger children in a family are sometimes proud that an older brother has gone to jail. "People always say their brother or cousin is in jail, even if it's not true," a twelve-year-old girl explained. "They're saying you better not mess with them because when their relative gets out he'll have big muscles and beat you up." George Miller, who is facing five years in prison in Chicago for selling drugs, says doing time is no big deal:

All you hear around my house is somebody going to jail and somebody coming home. Steve is going, Ed's out. Karen's on probation. Mike just shot somebody and the police are looking for him and he ain't been out a week.

Men coming out of prison are often welcomed by neighborhood kids as a conquering hero. They admire the tattoos on his body and the muscles in his back and arms from lifting weights. "Many young brothers seem like they don't care if they go to prison," ex-convict Ted Russell observes. "They think it's macho, it gives them more rank out on the street." Mr. Russell said he also wanted the experience. His uncle had told him, "it was smooth in there, that doing time was a piece of cake."

So many young men are going to prison that the average age of

Prison cells.

men incarcerated at facilities such as East Jersey State Prison has dropped in the past ten years from twenty-seven to twenty-three. "When I first came to prison, there were very few young guys," Bob Thomas, a lifer, recalls. "Now the young guys outnumber the older guys."

For many juveniles, their life in crime often started with dropping out of school, drinking a little wine, smoking a little marijuana, and trying to impress older guys. Then the marijuana became coke or crack, the hooky turned to breaking and entering or armed robbery. "Before you know it, you're packing a gun," Frank Allen points out. "And when you have a gun, someday you'll want to use it. Maybe just for target practice on a roof somewhere. But maybe one day, you might have to use it to defend yourself against someone else or to keep from getting caught. Or maybe, if you're high on crack, you might try it out on a person because you're angry or you want to see what it's like to shoot somebody."

On the other hand, there are teenagers in prison who have not committed violent crimes. Jim Anders adds: "People think that you got to be a killer to do a life sentence. Or you got to have committed a number of serious crimes. The system doesn't work that way at all. A lot of guys who are in here are here because they were in the wrong place at the wrong time. I'm not saying they were angels. Some of them were undoubtedly wild. But others were not getting into any serious trouble when they found themselves faced with a homicide charge."

Charlie Herbert is a classic case of a young person being in the wrong place at the wrong time:

> **I was not a kid who got in trouble, but I was a troubled kid. I'd play hooky from school, smoke reefers, drink alcohol. My parents were seldom home. . . . The big thing in my life was partying. I used to hang out with these two older guys: Bryan and Fred. Bryan was**

seventeen and Fred eighteen. They liked to drink and party . . . so I used to hang out with them and do the same things. . . . One night we were going to this party at the Jersey shore and our car broke down and we had to walk. So when Bryan said, "Let's steal a car," we went along with it. . . . We're driving along and we're pretty high and we pass a store and Bryan says, "See that store—let's stick it up." So we argued over this and the older guy—Fred—said, "Okay, I'll stick it up if there are no bullets in the gun." So Bryan took the bullets out and Fred holds up the store and comes away with about a hundred bucks.

Now we're driving around and we buy a bag of marijuana from some high school kids but we have no papers and we go to a store to get papers. And Bryan says, "I'll get the papers." Fred and I wait for him in the car. The next thing I know I hear this pop and it sounds like a gun and I start the car to get out of there and Bryan comes running out and hops in the car and says, "I just shot a guy." . . . He threatened to kill us if we said anything about it to anyone.

Offered a chance to plea bargain for a thirty-year term, Charlie and his family decided to go to trial. Bryan had confessed to the killing. Charlie admitted to charges of robbery and car theft but maintained that he didn't know that Bryan had intended to hold up the second store, let alone kill anyone—or that the gun he had was loaded. The jury did not believe him. Found guilty of homicide, the judge sentenced Charlie to life in prison plus an additional twelve to eighteen years for the robberies, car theft, and arson. He was sixteen years old. This meant that he would have to serve at least twenty years before he could be considered eligible for parole.

Calvin Smith was only fourteen years old when he received a thirty year–to-life sentence for killing a man during a robbery:

When the judge gave me thirty years, he said, "Now I want you all on the street to hear what I'm saying and look what's being done." I buckled. I got weak in the legs. . . . But it still didn't dawn on me really. I thought maybe he was trying to scare me. But a year after, when my appeals started coming back, I began to realize it was for real.

Until then, I had done no crimes against people. I had done juvenile offenses: stolen cars, robbery. I was going with what I'd seen. I admired the style of the guys who had nice clothes, big cars, pretty women, guns, money. That was what was going down. I wanted to get it. I was going to take it.

For many teenagers with long sentences, reality sets in slowly. At first, they act in prison as if they were still on the outside. They hang out with their friends rather than work or go to school. When older guys try to counsel or help them, they do not listen. Bob Thomas recalls:

When I came to prison, . . . you couldn't tell me nothing. I was really wild. But there were many older guys who would help out young kids like myself. They would push books on him, get him to get an education, take religion seriously, and keep in contact with his family. They would also protect you from other guys who might prey on you and try to take something from you, your possessions or your manhood. Today, there are so many young people in jail that it's not the same. Many guys don't want to hear about school and stuff

like that. At least, not now, not in the beginning. But sooner or later they'll settle down.

For a young prisoner coming into jail for the first time, prison is a terrifying experience. Mustafa Ali remembers his first day:

Your heart beats faster. Guys are looking down at you from their cells. They call out to you. These people are killers. They killed ten people, you think. They can do that to their mothers, their kid brothers, their loved ones. Imagine what they will do to you. . . . I had to prepare myself to do whatever I had to do. If they come to hurt me, or do some bodily harm to me, that meant I have to be prepared to do something to them before they did it to me. My attitude was not to come to jail to get a reputation. I always had a dream to go home.

The most feared form of violence in jail is sexual violence. Henry George remembers his first encounter with that threat:

I was really devastated the first time I was locked up. I was scared. I had heard all sorts of stories about what guys will do to you. There was a guy by the name of Henry. He used to come in and give me candy and pies and stuff. I thought he was just being nice. Then one Sunday morning, he told me, "Stay back in your cell this morning." I said, "For what?" He said, "Look, punk! You know what this is. I didn't give you those pies and all just because I'm your momma. Stay back in your cell!" I was like trembling. I was a country boy and I didn't understand those things. . . . So I told one of the guys I knew and he said, "Man, kill that

sucker." So he got me a razor blade. He said, "When the doors open, don't say nothing, but go right to his cell and kill him." I was so struck with fear that when the doors opened, I couldn't move. The guy then came into my cell and he hit me right in the face—boom! And I was so angry, that I began cutting into him. I cut into his face, his chest, everywhere. Fear was making me do that. I was shaking with fear. And anger. He seemed like such a good guy. He was nice to me. I really didn't expect that.

Most prisoners testify that the worst part of prison is not the violence but the waste. When the commanding officer of a prison was asked about rehabilitation, he sneered and replied, "You know how we rehabilitate people here? We make old men out of them."

Is there rehabilitation in prison? Some men in prison truly change their lives for the better. But there is always a certain degree of futility in accomplishing something behind bars, unless there is the opportunity to put the acquired skills and knowledge into practice in the real world. As a result, some psychologists feel that long prison terms are counterproductive. They maintain that as far as punishment is concerned, less is best. The mild punishment communicates the message that rules must be obeyed. In a recent study of five hundred juveniles held in a detention facility, 80 percent felt that fifteen to forty-five minutes of lockup was sufficient for them to get the message.

One prison psychologist who has worked with teenagers notes:

Nearly every inmate I ever interviewed at length has been brutally beaten as a child by his father, step father, or other power figure. Everything we call crime is a stupid, mismanaged, pitiful struggle by angry kids to get revenge in the most evil way they can.

Can we guide youngsters in a better direction to make life better and more productive? Keith Clark, a teenager on his way to prison, had one suggestion. "Instead of building prisons, they should be building factories," he said, holding up his wristwatch with "Made in China" printed on the back. "Let's build a watch factory. Give the people some jobs. Give them some way out."

9

DEATH FOR JUVENILES?

The United States is one of only seven countries in the world that continues to execute juveniles. Since colonial days, 282 juveniles have been executed in this country. The first recorded juvenile execution took place in 1642, when a sixteen-year-old boy was executed. Since then, almost three hundred males have been executed for crimes committed under the age of eighteen. The youngest child to be executed was about eleven, an unnamed black child who was hanged in Alexandria, Louisiana, in September 1855. James Arcene, a Cherokee Indian, was hanged as an adult at Fort Smith Arkansas in 1885 for a crime he had committed when he was ten years old.

One of the youngest children executed in twentieth-century America was fourteen-year-old George Junius Stinney, Jr., a black youth, electrocuted in South Carolina in 1944. He was executed two months after being convicted for the murders of two white children, Betty June Bonnicker and Mary Emma Thomas, ages eleven and eight. The girls had gone bicycling to pick flowers and when they failed to return, a search party found their bodies. They had been beaten to death. A few hours later, George Stinney was arrested and charged with the murders. According to the sheriff and Stinney's lawyer, Stinney confessed to both killings. It took ten minutes for the jury to find him guilty with no recommendation of mercy.

Stinney's lawyer, Charles Plowden, could have filed an appeal which would have at least delayed Stinney's death sentence for a year. He did not. Plowden later defended himself by saying that the family did not have the money to file an appeal. But many believe the real reason was that Plowden was running for a local office and did not want to antagonize voters. Despite the fact that the South had a history of executing blacks, many Southerners were shocked that a fourteen-year-old child was to be executed. One man wrote to the governor from Atlanta, Georgia:

> **I am a White Man. Now I am pleading with you for the life of a little Negro boy age fourteen that killed the two little white girls. A sentence in prison would be fair for the Negro boy. Please governor, try to save this boy's life.**

But the governor could not afford to be soft on "the race issue." On June 14, at eleven P.M., Stinney began his walk to the death chamber. When he entered the room he seemed calm. His arms were so thin, the guards had difficulty strapping them to the electric chair. A mask was lowered over George's face. The warden of the prison then signaled the executioner to pull the switch. The first jolt of 2,400 volts of electric current passed through Stinney's body. The death mask slipped from his face and his eyes were open when two additional jolts of electricity were added. James Gamble, the sheriff's seventeen-year-old son, who later became a state policeman, stood next to his father during the execution. Years later, he recalled his reaction to Stinney's execution:

> **It had a lot of effect on me. For a long time I turned against electrocution, period. I think the death penalty is proper in its place. But I don't think a fourteen-year-old boy should be electrocuted. I didn't then and I don't today.**

Americans generally have been reluctant to execute girls under the age of eighteen. The first known lawful execution of a female juvenile under eighteen for a crime on American soil took place on February 9, 1767, in New York, when a black teenager was hung for breaking into a house and stealing. The youngest girl ever to be executed was twelve-year-old Hannah Ocuisi, hanged on December 20, 1786. Hannah was found guilty of murdering six-year-old Eunice Bolles, in revenge for Eunice telling that Hannah had forcibly taken some strawberries from her. Despite Hannah's youth, her limited mental abilities, and her brutal life as a child, the judge decreed that she "be carried to the place of execution and there be hanged with a rope by the neck, between the heavens and the earth, until you are dead, dead, dead."

The Reverend Henry Channing of Yale College gave a sermon on the execution, calling Hannah's death sentence "a tremendous sentence which puts a period to the life of one who had never learned to live."

For the next 126 years, nine other girls under the age of eighteen were executed, nine by hanging and one by electrocution. The last teenage girl executed was Virginia Christian, a poor fifteen-year-old black girl who was executed in the state of Virginia in 1912. The teenager worked as a laundress for Mrs. Ida Virginia Belote, a white woman. Belote accused Virginia of stealing a shirt from the laundry. During an argument, Mrs. Belote struck Virginia with a metal object and Virginia, in a rage, struck back and eventually suffocated Mrs. Belote. She was sentenced to death even though it was clear that the killing was not premeditated but took place in a moment of rage. Virginia's supporters asked, "Why has it [the state of Virginia] not a law forbidding the execution of children under sixteen?" There was no answer then and there is none today. Almost two-thirds of the states continue to execute teenagers. And leading the group is the state of Texas, where today over ten youths are on death row in Huntsville for crimes they committed when under eighteen.

A thick fog clings to the death row unit—known as Ellis 1—at Huntsville State Prison in Huntsville, Texas, a town located between Dallas and Houston. Around the building, hidden in mists, prison guards, mounted on horseback, rifles in hand, keep watch. Inside death row, Gary Graham, prisoner number 686, has received official notice that shortly after midnight on August 17, 1993, he will be executed. All that stands between him and death is the Texas State Parole Board.

Several months earlier, the United States Supreme Court, in a 5 to 4 decision, voted to allow the state of Texas to execute him, despite the fact that there is a great deal of doubt whether or not he committed the crime for which he has been sentenced to death. If Gary Graham is executed, he will be one of more than 16,000 Americans executed in America in the past 300 years. The United

The Ellis 1 or Death Row unit at Huntsville, Texas.

States is, in fact, the execution capital of the Western world. More than 2,600 defendants presently wait on death rows throughout the country to be electrocuted, hanged, shot, gassed, or given lethal injections. About 200 more are sentenced to death every year and 20 to 30 are executed.

In 1981, Gary, then 17 years old, was in jail for a robbery charge, awaiting trial, when suddenly the police entered his cell and placed him in a police lineup without any explanation. His attorney later informed him that he had been identified by a woman who claimed to have seen him shoot Bobby Grant Lambert in a Safeway parking lot in Houston during an attempted robbery. She stated she was in her car, with two of her three children in the back seat, waiting for her third daughter to make a purchase inside the store. She claimed she noticed a black man walk up to a middle-class white man coming out of a supermarket, attempt to rob, and then shoot him. She also testified that she tried to chase the robber, leaving her three children behind and ignoring the man on the street.

Other people testified that, although they witnessed the killing, they could not identify Gary Graham as the attacker. In fact, eleven other witnesses have sworn that he was not the killer, but their testimony came thirty days after the trial. Texas law states that new evidence must be presented within thirty days of a conviction in order to be valid. It was this law that the Supreme Court upheld.

Gary Graham says he makes no excuses for his life on the streets. "I had a mother in a mental institution. My father was in prison. I lived with different relatives. I didn't have a stable background. I was manipulated by older kids into drug abuse, which led to robbery." He did plead guilty to robbing and assaulting ten people in a six-day crime spree. "I was into street life and all of that. But I did not murder anyone," Gary Graham insists emphatically.

Today, in Ellis 1 in Huntsville, teenagers are regularly sentenced to death. Gary Graham is but one of several men on death row for crimes committed as teenagers. With him is Lionel Rodriguez, who at the age of nineteen, was convicted of killing twenty-two-year-old Tracy Gee of Houston, Texas, in 1990, because his car was low on gas and he wanted hers. Rodriguez makes no excuses. "My lifestyle, my way of thinking got me here," he says:

> **At the age of eleven, I hung around with "the bad boys," getting high, skipping school. When I was 15, I took my stepfather's car without permission. He was a policeman. He had me picked up. I wouldn't listen to anyone. All the time, I was getting high, chasing girls. I skipped school all day, riding around. I chose my friends over my family. I was living for myself. Wake up, take a shower, eat, get high, sleep, drink, sleep**

Gary Graham has been on death row for almost 14 years. He was convicted for murder when he was 17. Graham denies having committed the crime.

with chicks who would sleep with you. . . . Selling drugs. In and out of prison. It was looking through a cloud. You can't see anything in front of you. Once you fall it's the bottom of the trash can of society.

Rodriguez says that he was indifferent to his fate and was not even mentally present at his trial. When he was sentenced to death, he says, "I shook my attorney's hand and thanked him. The verdict didn't even shock me."

Lionel Rodriguez, like all Texas prisoners sentenced to death, was immediately transferred to the special unit which houses death row inmates. He lives in a five-by-nine-foot cell, eats regular meals, and is allowed to watch television and receive books, magazines, and legal materials. Daily life here is, in many ways, no different than the routine in the rest of the prison. Prisoners work five hours a day, five days a week and are allowed recreation three hours a day, five days a week. There are courses available and visits. But there are some differences. Men on death row are not allowed to mix with the rest of the prison population. Nor is there any privacy. The cell has bars and guards check on prisoners regularly. Letters are opened and read. For those condemned men who refuse to work, which they can do, they are confined to their cells most of the day with limited exercise privileges.

After arriving on death row, Rodriguez gradually became aware of the meaningless life that he and others like him were leading in prison.

Almost everybody's looking at TV eighteen hours a day. They're living in escapism. One time the power got shut off. No TV. No radio. No nothing. You know what happened? You ever been in a zoo when you got to see the monkeys in cages? You know how they're running around, hollering at each other? Same thing.

Reality kicked in. All these guys were yelling at each other. . . . They didn't want to deal with reality. Reality was right there in their face. When all the power came back on everything got real quiet.

To face death takes great courage, and many men turn to God. For Lionel Rodriguez, faith became the answer to his life. "If you're not Christ-centered, your life is not stable. Any change is not going to last. A person needs to commit his life to Christ." The man who turned him on to being a Christian was another condemned man, Mark Fronckiewicz, who at one time boasted, "I used to turn these kids into killers."

Mark Fronckiewicz is a man for whom crime and trouble were a

Lionel Rodriguez has been on death row for a year, time enough, he says, for him to have found God.

way of life from the time he was eleven. He was in and out of jail four times before he was accused of a murder-for-hire in prison in a gang-related prison murder. Fronckiewicz claims that he is being framed for this particular crime even while admitting his life has been filled with one criminal activity after another:

> **I'm here on death row for being head of one of the most vicious groups of men in the whole state. I don't deny any of it. I was a man filled with hate. I hated everything around me. I had no sense of identity. I'm a career criminal. I can understand society telling me you can't live in society no more. We're going to kill you.**

Mark Fronckiewicz was turned on to religion in prison by "a guy who I respected as a criminal":

> **I had it preached to me all my life and I always said, "Yeah, yeah, yeah." But I was at the end of my rope. I had been in segregation for a year. They stopped all my visits. They had cut me loose. I had nothing. They crushed my whole world. I brought it all crashing down on me. I thought I could beat them at their own game. And I couldn't. They put me in isolation.**

His encounter with the Bible led him to discover a new way of life:

> **It brought something in my life that can answer a lot of questions. Not a day goes by that I don't struggle with it. But I know there's a better way to do things. I told God, ". . . I'm not going to ask you to get me out of here. I want something real small. I just want you**

to bring somebody into my life that I can talk to about a lot of things. . . ." The next day I got this letter from a minister. Ever since then I've never turned back. It's been hard. Don't get me wrong. . . . Not a day goes by that I don't struggle with it. But I know there's something better.

What disturbs Mark Fronckiewicz is the number of teenagers he sees on death row every year. It really bothers him to see eighteen- and nineteen-year-olds being executed. He wonders what they are being killed for. Gary Graham says he shares Mark's feelings about executing teenagers.

It sends a message to our children: This is the way we deal with conflict. We simply eliminate individuals . . . and solve our problems. We see the same old cycles repeated over and over again. And the crime waves continue. We have over 2,600 people on death row. If we executed all of them in the morning, the public would be no safer.

Gary feels the answer to juvenile crime lies in restoring and redeeming the individual. He asks, "Can teenagers, due to their inherent maturity, impulsiveness and lack of full appreciation of the consequences of their acts, ever be in that very worst category, and thus be deserving of the death sentence?" His answer is no, because people have the ability to change. He uses himself as an example:

I have changed since being on death row. And I think if you take any individual and take him off of drugs, he's automatically going to change. Children may get into very bad situations which they don't have the emotional and intellectual ability to deal with things.

. . . **But as they mature, as they grow, they become more conforming to behavioral patterns.**

What we need is punishment but also treatment. Really work with these individuals. The individual who commits a crime, he doesn't feel a part of a family. He becomes detached from the family unit. And he has to be restored. He has to be shown that someone out there actually cares. That the community is a part of him and we are part of each other.

The condemned go through more psychological changes than any other prisoners. For some the worst part is in the waiting. Charles Rumbaugh, who sat with Gary, Mark, and Lionel on death row, once remarked:

Waiting for the appeal court can get to you. I feel like I've been traveling down a long, dark, winding tunnel for the past nine years and now I can see no end to the tunnel. . . . I have reached the point where I no longer care. I'm so . . . tired and disgusted with sitting here and watching my friends take the final trip to the execution chamber, while I sit and wait and speculate about when my time will come. They kill me a little each day. To me, the dying is the easy part. It's the waiting and not knowing that's hard.

Rumbaugh finally stopped his appeals. He was executed.

While many men continue to hope for a reprieve to the last minute, some prepare to die. Lionel Rodriguez finds he can prepare himself with faith. He says that he has made peace with himself and is willing to accept whatever happens:

I'm content. If they give it to us, they give it to us. If they don't, they don't. I want others to know that I've changed. When I realized how wretched I was, I was a sick person. Now, I've accepted Christ. Now I thank God that I'm here and I realize reality. This is a life and death situation. You don't know when you're going to die. The most important thing is getting your heart straight with God.

But Lionel is aware that many men on death row, unwilling to face the reality of their lives, will complain to the very end that they are a victim of circumstances:

And even people who say I didn't do this crime, still it has something to do with your lifestyle. Teenagers out there saying, "Sure I smoke, I drink, but I don't play with guns. I be careful when I drive. I don't speed." That person could still end up here, very easily. He might say, "I ended up in the wrong place at the wrong time," but I tell him, "No, your lifestyle got you here. It's time to deal with it, look and accept it, and say, 'What now?' " That's the turning point of your life.

If either Gary Graham, Mark Fronckiewicz, or Lionel Rodriguez is executed, the procedure will be like this:

Shortly before the day of the execution, the prisoner is transferred from Ellis 1 to the Walls Unit—the house of death. The move is made in secrecy to prevent any rescue attempts. The trip is about fifteen miles and takes twenty minutes. After he is transported, the condemned man may receive visits from friends, family, a legal representative, and a minister until six o'clock on the evening of his execution. Only his minister is allowed to remain with him until the moment of death. Between six-thirty and seven o'clock, the last meal

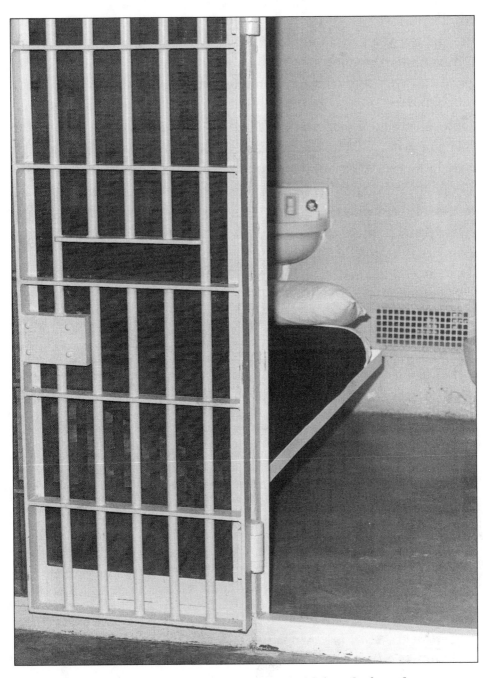

This is the cell in which prisoners are held just before they are executed.

will be served. Out of the sixty executions that have taken place in the last ten years, ten men have refused to take any food. One man, Carlos Santana, asked for "justice, temperance with mercy" for his last meal. They were not on his menu. David Clark, executed in 1992, told officials he was fasting. Some men ask for something simple such as an apple or yogurt. Mexican prisoners have asked for Hispanic food. Other prisoners ask for more traditional dishes such as hamburgers, pizza, chicken, and steak. The largest meal eaten by a condemned man in recent times was by Ronald O'Brian, executed in 1984. He consumed a T-bone steak, french fries with catsup, corn, sweet peas, lettuce and tomato salad with egg and French dressing, ice tea, saltines, ice cream, Boston cream pie, and rolls.

The condemned man is required to be clean and neat for his exe-

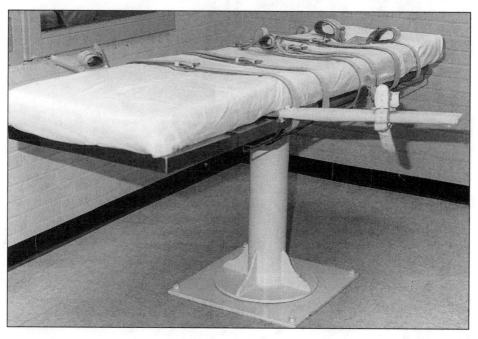

A condemned man is strapped to this gurney just before the lethal injection is administered.

cution. Shortly before midnight, he showers and changes into freshly laundered clothes. Meanwhile, a medical technician, not a doctor, prepares a lethal injection consisting of panuronium bromide (a muscle relaxant), and lethal doses of two chemicals, potassium chloride and sodium thiopental.

Witnesses to the execution, including friends, family, and press, assemble at eleven forty-five in the lounge adjacent to the visiting room. Shortly after midnight, the door is unlocked and the condemned man is removed from his holding cell and strapped into a gurney, a lightweight mobile hospital bed used by ambulance crews to transport patients, and wheeled into the execution room. The medical technician inserts an intravenous catheter into the condemned man's arm. A neutral saline solution begins to flow into his body. The saline solution has no overt physical effect but makes it easier to administer the lethal dose when the time comes. The witnesses are then assembled to see him executed.

Throughout this process, telephone lines are kept open directly to the execution chamber if, for any reason, a stay is ordered by the courts. When the appointed hour of execution arrives, the warden of the prison asks the condemned man if he has a last statement. Some men die asking forgiveness for their crimes. Others claim their innocence and protest the injustice of their execution. Some are silent; others, hostile. Many express their love for their family, wives, friends, and sweethearts.

After the last statement is made by the prisoner, the warden then announces, "We are ready." The medical technician, who is hidden from the witnesses and the condemned man by a wall and locked door, administers the lethal injection through the catheter. The poison enters the prisoner's body. A brief convulsion, a gasping for breath, and then blackness.

Seconds later, a prisoner is dead.

CONCLUSION

The law enforcement statistics tell a grim tale. Over 100,000 juveniles are arrested for violent crimes, including murder, forcible rape, and aggravated assault. Another 90,000 are arrested for drug offenses and 700,000 for property crimes, including burglary, theft, and larceny. While 78 percent of those arrested are white, over 50 percent of those in prison are black. In addition to the known figures, there are the millions of young people who suffer from sexual abuse, drug and alcohol addiction, who run away from home, or drop out of society altogether, and end up as part of America's homeless population.

There is no great mystery as to why so many young people throughout America are in trouble. Something has gone wrong with their families. As many as 70 percent of juvenile offenders came from single-parent homes. They grow up in neighborhoods where violence is an everyday occurrence. The result, as one psychologist has pointed out, is generation after generation of violent children:

> We know that children with an early history of serious criminal and deviant behavior who attack, rape, rob, and sometimes kill are alienated and hostile, with antisocial values and attitudes, unwilling or unable to control themselves. And that they come from backgrounds that seem to support this criminal behavior; that they have inadequate parents, their role models are from the street, and they have no connections to family, school or church, or socializing institutions of society. They lack conscience, maturity, character, insight, empathy, and verbal skills.

A young woman calls the Covenant House Nine Line to find out where she can get help in her community.

Juveniles become runaway or throwaway kids, drug addicts, prostitutes, robbers, drug dealers, and gunmen because they often come from families where parents have the same background. Even if a parent is caring, many cannot control their children or compete with the pressures and temptations of the fast life on the street.

Juveniles in trouble are America's unwanted children. Some are children brought into this world unwanted and unloved by their parents. Antisocial or criminal behavior is often a response to their circumstances. Others are unwanted by a society that fears them and often despises them.

What is the solution? Some observers say tougher laws and harsher penalties. There is no evidence to support this position. Sending juveniles to jail for a long time usually ensures that they will lead a life of crime. Once a young person is incarcerated with experienced criminals, he or she usually winds up an experienced criminal.

Nor does the death penalty make young people stop and think before killing someone. Charles Rumbaugh, who was executed for killing a jeweler in a holdup when he was a teenager, dismissed the notion. "I was seventeen years old when I committed the offense for which I was sentenced to die, and I didn't even start thinking about my life until I was twenty." Most juveniles who kill do so impulsively or because they are driven by intense emotional feelings. Few think about the consequences of their act.

Since the basic reason why juveniles get in trouble is because they come from troubled families, the goal of those who work with them is to find a way to replace the family. They believe that the overwhelming majority of young people in trouble are not lost, even those who are dangerous. Many troubled young people, given professional care and treatment, have developed into productive human beings. They have learned a skill, found a job, earned a good living, and raised a family.

Often the degree of success depends upon how old the children are when they receive help. The younger they are, the better the chances of helping them straighten out their lives. Judge Michael Corriero feels that social agencies should start intervening when a child is three and four years old. In Judge Corriero's view, sixteen may be too late. Philip Dobbs, supervising Probation officer for the New York City Department of Probation, has seen thousands of juveniles in trouble throughout his career. He has worked successfully with older teenagers in an intense program in which counselors provided constant care and supervision to small groups of young people. Dobbs notes:

A Covenant House volunteer supplies all callers in trouble with the names, addresses, and phone numbers of city and private agencies in the caller's area where help can be obtained.

Some teenagers do well in a program as long as that program lasts. If you show a kid you truly care for him, if you're willing to go the extra mile, if you are willing to make yourself available when he needs you, then you may be able to turn a kid around. But they cannot stay in a program forever. They will need structure for a good part of their life so that don't fall back into the old ways of doing things. You can't give up on a kid even if he has given up on himself. But you can't save a kid unless he wants to save himself.

For juveniles in trouble or for their families who need help, Covenant House offers a free referral service to the nearest social agency for assistance. Their number is 1-800-999-9999.

BIBLIOGRAPHY

Baker, Falcon. *Saving Our Kids: From Delinquency, Drugs and Despair*. New York: Cornelia and Michael Bessie Books, 1991.

Bing, Léon. *Do or Die*. New York: HarperPerennial, 1991.

Brown, Claude. *Manchild in the Promised Land*. New York: Signet Books, 1965.

Ritter, Bruce. *Sometimes God Has a Kid's Face*. New York: Covenant House, 1988.

_____.*Covenant House: Lifeline to the Streets*. New York: Doubleday, 1987.

Shakur, Sanyika. *Monster: The Autobiography of an L.A. Gang Member*. New York: Grove/Atlantic Monthly Press, 1993.

Streib, Victor. *Death Penalty for Juveniles*. Bloomington: Indiana University Press, 1989.

Williams, Terry. *The Cocaine Kids: The Inside Story of a Drug Ring*. Reading, MA: Addison-Wesley, 1989.

INDEX